GODLY WISDOM

FOR

PROSPERITY

by

Jerry Savelle

HARRISON HOUSE
P.O. Box 35035
Tulsa, Okla. 74135

(All Scripture quotations from the *King James Version* of the Bible unless otherwise stated.)

ISBN 0-89274-158-9
Printed in the United States of America
Copyright © 1980 Jerry Savelle
All Rights Reserved

Table of Contents

Preface 5

Chapter 1
Set Goals For Your Life 9

Chapter 2
Meet the Conditions 19

Chapter 3
Seeking and Finding Wisdom 29

Chapter 4
Finding Godly Wisdom Involves Work 35

Chapter 5
The Need for Discipline 41

Chapter 6
Find — Get — Lay Hold — Retain 49

Chapter 7
Guidelines for Prosperity 57

Chapter 8
Prosperity is Progressive 67

Chapter 9
Borrowing Money — Is It Wrong? 75

Chapter 10
The Believer and Easy Credit 79

Chapter 11
The Christian and Credit Cards 89

Chapter 12
Get the Pressure Off and Your Word Level Up 93

Chapter 13
Beware of Deception 97

Chapter 14
Follow God's Instructions 105

Chapter 15
Be One of The Rare Kind 111

Chapter 16
Learn to Give 117

Chapter 17
Learn to Receive 123

Chapter 18
Occupy 127

Chapter 19
Become a Faithful Steward 135

Chapter 20
Storehouses..................................... 139

Chapter 21
Learning to Use Your Faith 145

Chapter 22
If You're Faithful to God's Storehouse,
He is Faithful to Yours 151

Preface

Most Christians desire to prosper but so many lack the wisdom that is necessary to produce it. God's people are destroyed because of a lack of knowledge. Some don't even know that it is God's will that they prosper. On the other hand, some know that prosperity belongs to them but haven't realized the importance of using wisdom.

There are laws that govern prosperity. We will discuss these laws briefly, but the aim of this book is to teach you how to apply God's wisdom for prosperity.

You may have to go *back to the basics* in order to completely understand *Godly Wisdom for Prosperity*. You may say, "Oh, I already know all about prosperity." Well, is what you know working for you?

The apostle Peter wrote in one of his letters, ". . . I will not be negligent to put you always in remembrance of these things, though ye know them, and be established in the present truth. Yea, I think it meet, as long as I am in this tabernacle, to stir you up by putting you in remembrance" (2 Peter 1:12, 13). There are some things that I have learned over the years from God's Word that I need to have brought to my remembrance. We should never forget the basics.

If you have not been acting upon the Word as you once did, you should begin to do so immediately. You may be faced with a crisis and think, "Oh, God! I have to have a great, new revelation to get me out of this jam."

The Spirit of God will speak to you and say, "Go back to the basics." You never leave the basics; you build upon them.

May I point out that it would be vain for a contractor or builder to destroy the foundation once it is laid. You do not destroy foundations; you build upon them.

The house is only as strong as its foundation. I believe that it is important that I share with you, not only in this section of the book, but in every chapter, the basics for building your foundation for prosperity. Your foundation may have some cracks in it, or it may be weak; you may have absolutely destroyed it. But I believe by the time you finish this study it will be secure and solid. Thank God, the Bible tells us that the floods and storms of life cannot shake the man who has his house built on a solid foundation. I desire a solid foundation. How about you?

Most people want to prosper but they are lacking the wisdom to do so, and therefore they do things that are unwise. If you can get to the place where your ways are God's ways, and you think like God thinks, you will have prosperity. I have never known God to fail or to make an unwise investment, have you?

I said this through the Spirit of God several years ago: "Lord, if I could just learn to think like You, I would never be faced with lack. I would never be faced with want, and I would never be faced with a crisis that I could not handle."

He said to me, "Well, Son, that is the reason I inspired the Scriptures." *The thoughts of God are in His Book*! It tells us what God thinks about life; what He thinks about healing; what He thinks about wealth and riches, and what He thinks about you and me. What God thinks about everything that you and I are involved in is all in the Book. God covered it all in sixty-six volumes!

People need to realize that the Bible is the greatest book ever written on the subject of prosperity. Let us go to God's Word and see what He says for us to do in order to obtain *Godly Wisdom for Prosperity*.

1
Set Goals For Your Life

The Bible says that without a vision the people perish. A vision does not necessarily mean a divine appearance of God, His Son, or an angelic being. A vision is simply a goal: an objective; something that motivates you; something that you can aim for. You must have goals in your life. You must have objectives. People who do not have goals or objectives are people without motivation. And people without motivation are people who are non-productive. Non-productive people perish.

I was driving through a little town once, and God pointed something out to me that I would like to share at this time. It was one of those little places where if you blinked your eyes you went right through the town without even realizing it. I saw a sign giving the name of the town, and I thought that I was approaching the city limits when suddenly there was another sign that said, "You have just left the city limits of . . . ."

I thought, "Wait a minute! I didn't even get to see it!" I backed up and I was right in the middle of town. There was a store on one side of the road, and another store on the other side. One store was called, "a mercantile." It was a general store. You could buy almost anything there. In fact, that store was like one of those cartoons that you have probably seen, where the same person just changed hats for each job that he performed. The post office, the sheriff's office, and the justice of the peace: every civic duty was performed in that one little store.

I wanted to buy a cold drink and get out of the routine of driving to just relax for awhile. As I looked around I saw a few shabby houses here and there. The structure of that drab old mercantile store was terrible. Apparently it had not been repaired for quite some time. It had not been painted or had a board replaced in years. The gas pumps in front of the building were out of date. I had to watch where I stepped because of the loose boards. Some of them were even missing. I could just barely straddle the framework of that porch.

Five men were sitting there playing checkers. They didn't even have enough motivation to turn around and say, "May I help you?" I am not criticizing their intelligence, but I am saying that they had absolutely no motivation — no drive. As I walked up on that porch, all I heard was, "It's your move."

I thought, "Here is a group of people who have no vision, no motivation." There was only one thing to do in that town — to become the *"Checker King!"* They didn't even have enough motivation to do something about the condition of their town. Why? They had no vision.

It's Your Move!

Many Christians are like the people in that little town. They want prosperity, good health, and the blessings of God, but they have no motivation. I want you to know that the Gospel is a victorious message. It will change your life. God's Word is full of "good news." The men who lived by the covenant of God were the wealthiest people on the face of the earth.

Everybody in his right mind wants prosperity. But the problem is, there are a lot of believers who haven't enough motivation to do what it takes to get prosperity. If you have the idea that *the message of faith* is some kind of *get-rich-quick-deal*, you can just forget it. In fact, I'll just pass this on to you right now: if anybody presents you with any kind of *get-rich-quick-deal*, please check it out GOOD! Because is is probably illegal. *Living by faith in the Word of God is not some kind of get-rich-quick-deal.* However, I will tell you what it will do for the one who makes it a way of life. It will change the condition of his bank account, his clothes, his automobile, his home, and it will change everything around him.

Prosperity does not come to you automatically. *You* must have a goal; *you* must have a vision; *you* must be motivated. *You* are going to have to make up *your* mind and say, "I'll do anything within the boundaries of God's Word to get it."

It's your move! You set that goal! And the first thing that I am going to ask you to do is write it down — NOW! *Underline it;* keep it before your eyes.

I have found in my own life, that if I write things down purposely, either in my Bible or in a notebook, and keep them in front of me, and never forget where they are found, then I keep my vision strong and active. When the devil comes in and tries to destroy my goal through pressure, crisis, or some kind of adverse circumstances, I can flip back over to where I wrote it down, and read it again. That strengthens my vision or goal.

You will find that in order to prosper, there are certain demands you will have to make on yourself. Regardless of your past failures, set that goal. Did you know that a lot of sinners, businessmen who could not care less whether Jesus of Nazareth is dead or alive, have succeeded in business because they had a vision? They set a goal.

There are men who have written books, taking biblical principles and applying them (although they were sinners), and they have worked for them. Many have written books on positive thinking, motivation, and how to succeed. They have taken the Scripture: "As a man thinketh in his heart, so is he . . ." and built an empire out of that. If carnal minded men can lay hold upon this spiritual law and make it work, then it is a shame if Christians don't do likewise.

Please do not misunderstand. I am not looking to build an empire. I am after what rightfully belongs to me through the shed blood of the Lord Jesus Christ. Money means absolutely nothing to me personally. As far as being able to walk around with money hanging out of my pockets, I could not care less. But I do intend to live the way that the Bible says I can. I have a right to have abundance, lacking nothing. My needs should be met and much left over to help someone else.

You may have already set some goals for your life, but you allowed them to become distorted. Or, you may not have known up until now that prosperity is available to you. Regardless of your situation I want you to approach this study as though you have never heard any teaching on prosperity. Allow the Word to inspire you.

ALWAYS ALLOW YOUR GOAL, YOUR VISION, OR YOUR OBJECTIVE TO AGREE WITH GOD'S WORD.

Get into God's Word and let it create your goal for you. The beautiful thing about this is God's Word is not void of power. If His Word says it, you have the right to make it your goal. If you follow the instructions in God's Word, He will back it. He will see to it that it is not just a dream. Many people are just chasing dreams because they are not in agreement with God's Word. Others will say, "Well, I just don't know if it is God's will that I prosper."

Well! Let's go to the Word of God and see what it says about prosperity being the will of God.

When God began to deal with me about *Godly Wisdom for Prosperity*, I began to read all the Scriptures concerning prosperity as though I had never read them before. I began to pick up things from the Spirit of God. One of the things that I received in my spirit was this: *"Prosperity is for the Believer!"*

I read this in 1 Kings 2:1-3: "Now the days of David drew nigh that he should die; and he charged Solomon his son, saying, I go the way of all the earth: be thou strong therefore, and shew thyself a man; And keep the charge of the Lord thy God, to walk in his ways, to keep his statutes, and his commandments, and his judgments, and his testimonies, as it is written in the law of Moses, that thou mayest prosper in all that thou doest, and whithersoever thou turnest thyself."

Now I realized that David was speaking to his son, Solomon, but I also knew that the apostle Paul actually said the same thing when he prayed in Colossians 1:9, 10: "For this cause we also, since the day we heard it, do not cease to pray for you, and to desire that ye might be filled with the knowledge of his will in all wisdom and spiritual understanding; That ye might walk worthy of the Lord unto all pleasing, *being fruitful in every good work*, and increasing in the knowledge of God." Being fruitful is prosperity. Paul said, "... *being fruitful in every good work.*" *Not some of them; not many of them; not a good percentage of them; not win-a-few — lose-a-few*, but in EVERY GOOD WORK. Paul, by the inspiration of the Holy Spirit, is telling us that God has made prosperity available to His people, and David told Solomon that if he would follow the instructions he would not only prosper in whatever he did, but wherever he went.

I began to think about that, and I said, "Wait a minute! I know that I have a right to prosper in everything I do, and wherever I go, but there are some things that I have done, and I did not prosper. I have been in some places where I did not prosper." Yes! I have *blown it* a few times! *Now, I'm not going to tell you just how many times that I have made mistakes, but there have been a few times in which I did not deal wisely.* I knew that I had the right to prosper, but I did not prosper because of unwise actions and it proved to be very costly.

WHAT ABOUT YOU?

God may have given you a goal and when you got it you thought, "Praise the Lord! This is what I've been looking for." But, you lacked wisdom in how to achieve your goal and the next thing you knew you had no motivation and thought, "What's the use in going on?"

Evidently, you needed *godly wisdom*. God's Word not only promises prosperity for believers in whatever we do and wherever we go, but He also will make available to us the wisdom in how to get it done.

Many times people have laid hold upon the fact that they have a right to prosper, but they lack the wisdom in how to do it. They fouled it up so badly that they became discouraged. They stopped living by the Word, and they were deceived by the devil. I personally know people who, with all sincerity, made a decision to live by faith in God's Word, but they did not have the proper understanding or the godly wisdom necessary to live this way. They heard some man give his testimony, and thought they could do exactly what he did. They did not know what he had been doing in the background: the days and nights that he had stayed up, confessing the Word of God, and believing God for the wisdom of God to do it. The man had only one service in which to share his testimony, and he could only give the highlights. The next thing that happened, the people went out and tried to do what he did, and they fell flat on their faces. They did not understand why, so they gave up. Now they are deceived, and in worse shape than they ever were before. They need to get wisdom.

God has provided the ability for the Body of Christ to prosper in everything that we do, and wherever we go. But I guarantee you, it will not fall on you like apples off a tree. It takes wisdom, understanding, prudence, judgment, and discretion to get it done.

David told Solomon to keep the charge of the Lord: to walk in God's ways, to keep His statutes, and His commandments, His judgments, and His testimonies as it is written in the law of Moses; then he could prosper in all that he did, and wherever he went.

I want you to write these words down. *"This is my goal. This year I will prosper in whatever I do, and wherever I go."* Keep it before you at all times. Don't let that goal become distorted. Every opportunity you have to fail, get back into the Word of God and refresh your spirit with His Word. It is His will for you to prosper and be in health even as your soul prospers. (See 3 John 2.)

2
Meet the Conditions

Every promise of God is conditional. The Spirit of God once shared this with me, and my spirit rejoiced over it: "Son, did you ever stop to think why I put conditions to those promises?"

I said, "No, not really."

He said, "A promise, first of all, reveals My will. With every promise I make, I always put a condition. *The reason I put the condition there, is not to bind you — but to bind satan.* You see, once the condition is met, satan is bound by the Word."

Many people say, "Yes, but the condition is so hard. I don't know why God makes me do this. I know that the Bible says that He wills that I prosper and be in health even as my soul prospers, but I do not have time for my soul to prosper. I need money now. I don't know why God had to make this so hard."

If you talk like that, you need to know that the reason God put the condition in there is to bind the devil: to limit him. You see, *as long as the conditions are not met you are limited*. That gives the devil an open door to come in there and try to wipe you out. But, once you find the promise of God and you meet the conditions, and do it with the understanding that the door is closed on the devil, then he has no avenue in which he can get to you. You will prosper. You will win.

The conditions are not to bind God's people, but to put them in a position of advantage. I love meeting the conditions, because every time I see a condition and I do it, I can say, "Old devil, you are bound! You are finished and you cannot cross the line."

Somebody said, "Yes, I met the conditions and he still crossed the line." No, you haven't met all of the conditions. If you had, the devil would have fled from you.

The Bible says, "Submit yourselves therefore to God. Resist the devil, and he will flee from you" (James 4:7). God keeps His Word. When the condition is met, satan cannot cross the line. When God puts out His Word, He puts the condition that is necessary to fulfill that promise. When you meet that condition, satan is bound. When satan is bound, I want you to know God has an open door to pour out His blessings upon you. The blessings of God will come on you and overtake you.

There is no reason for you to wait until you get to heaven to receive the blessings of God. You won't have any problem with prosperity or satan when you get to heaven. Haven't you heard? The devil is not going to heaven. The time for prosperity is NOW. I don't know about you but I am not in any hurry to get to heaven, because I already know that I am going there.

Somebody said, "Oh! but don't you know the world is going to get worse? Don't you know what is being prophesied? Don't you know that the Body of Christ is going to be smothered and squashed?"

I know what the Bible says about that but, you see, I am one of the righteous. The Word says that the righteous will never be forsaken nor will they ever beg bread. Shortages, crises, and pressures do not frighten me because *I am one of the righteous.* I have a covenant with God. Please do not misunderstand; I am not saying that I ignore all of those things. *I acknowledge what the Word says.* Read Romans 8:31-39. We are more than conquerors through Christ Jesus.

I am not going to wait until I get to heaven to enjoy what is available to me NOW. I have a right to prosper in whatever I do and wherever I go.

I Had To Learn To Meet The Conditions

As I said before; there have been some times in my life when I did not prosper. I failed to meet the conditions. I said, "Lord, You said that I have a right to prosper in whatever I do and wherever I go, and You know that there have been times when I did not prosper."

He said, "Son, that is your fault, not mine. I have made prosperity available to you. The problem is you lack wisdom." We must all come to this realization: ANY FAILURE IS ON OUR PART, NOT GOD'S OR HIS WORD!

Without A Vision You Perish

In chapter one, I asked you to set a goal; to write it down, and to keep it before you. You may say, "Brother Jerry, there is no need for me to write my goal down on paper. You don't know my past. Oh! I have tried to set goals, and tried to set goals, and I just get worse every year. There is no need in me reading your book. I am just not a highly motivated person."

Well! GET MOTIVATED! I wasn't either, until I got hold of the Word of God. I had always taken a step backwards. I'll tell you what kind of discipline I had: I went through about six jobs the first year of my marriage. Why? Because if it got tough I would quit. Then — I got hold of the Word of God, and I found that if I wanted to live by faith I was going to have to change my ways. I found out quickly that it was going to take some discipline and some demands on myself. That is one reason that I love being a pastor now. The people's growth demands that I preach new insight to them, and that keeps me digging in the Word. You must get in the Word.

If ... If ... If ...

We shall read Deuteronomy 28:1, 2 "And it shall come to pass, *if thou shalt hearken diligently* unto the voice of the Lord thy God, to *observe* and to *do all his commandments* which I command thee this day, that the Lord thy God will set thee on high above all the nations of the earth: And all these blessings shall come on thee, and overtake thee, *if* thou shalt hearken unto the voice of the Lord thy God." Please read this again so you will have it fresh in your spirit. "And all these blessings shall come on thee, and overtake thee, if thou shalt hearken unto the voice of the Lord thy God." The key word is "if." This tells us the condition that must be met before the blessings can come.

Peter told us that he would not be negligent to put us always in remembrance of these things, even though we know them and have become established in them. (See 2 Peter 1:12) It never hurts to have your mind refreshed by the Scriptures. Let's read Galatians 3:13: "Christ hath redeemed us from the curse of the law, being made a curse for us: for it is written, Cursed is every one that hangeth on a tree." And verse 14 tells us, "That the blessing of Abraham might come on the Gentiles through Jesus Christ; that we might receive the promise of the Spirit through faith." Here, we are told that Christ has redeemed us from the curse of the law, and that Abraham's blessings are ours. Deuteronomy 28 begins to reveal to us, first of all, the promises or the blessings of Abraham. It also reveals in the latter part of the chapter, the curses of the law. We receive the blessings of Abraham through faith. *Faith is the condition that has to be met.* "IF" you operate in faith these blessings will overtake you.

You will remember that David spoke these words to Solomon: ". . . and he charged Solomon his son, saying, I go the way of all the earth: be thou strong therefore, and shew thyself a man; And keep the charge of the Lord thy God, to walk in his ways, to keep his statutes, and his commandments, and his judgments, and his testimonies, as it is written in the law of Moses, that thou mayest prosper in all that thou doest, and whithersoever thou turnest thyself" (1 Kings 2:1-3).

Did Solomon take David's advice? If he did, then did it produce results? We shall see.

There are some examples in the Bible where men did not meet the conditions (follow the instructions), and they were not blessed. But you will discover that when they realized where they missed it, and corrected it, then the blessings came. The apostle Paul was one. Paul *missed it* a few times. He was human, just like you and me. He compromised in some cases just like we have. However, Paul learned his lesson. He got back on God's Word, and his closing remarks were, "I kept the faith . . . and I fought a good fight . . . ."

That should be our closing remarks as the Spirit of God catches us away with the Lord Jesus Christ at His appearing; "I have kept the faith, and I fought a good fight. Praise the Lord!"

What About Solomon?

For the answer to that question, we go to 2 Chronicles 1:7-10: "In that night did God appear unto Solomon, and said unto him, Ask what I shall give thee. And Solomon said unto God, Thou hast shewed great mercy unto David my father, and hast made me to reign in his stead. Now, O Lord God, let thy promise unto David my father be established: for thou hast made me king over a people like the dust of the earth in multitude. Give me now wisdom and knowledge, that I may go out and come in before this people: for who can judge this thy people, that is so great?"

The Lord actually asked Solomon, "What can I do for you? What would you like?" and Solomon asked for wisdom and knowledge!

Somebody said, "I'll tell you: if God had appeared to me, I would not have asked for wisdom and knowledge. I would have said, 'Give me a million dollars!' "

Yes, and if God gave it to you, it would be gone in a month because you would not have the wisdom and knowledge in how to use it. If God gave a million dollars to most Christians, it would be gone in less than four weeks. They would be flat on their backs: bawling, squalling, begging, and saying, "God, why did You let this happen to me?"

Why? Because they lack wisdom. Anybody who has ever had a million dollars will tell you that it takes more knowledge and wisdom to keep it, than it did to make it. There is a *spiritual outlaw* out there (satan) who doesn't want that money spent for the *gospel's sake*. It is his nature to try to destroy it. There are many people whom satan has destroyed because of money.

There is nothing wrong with having money, but if your priorities are not right, if you lack wisdom, it will destroy you. *God is not telling you that you cannot have financial prosperity. But you need to realize that it takes the wisdom of God to put it to work in the proper channels, and to stay wealthy.* There is nothing wrong with owning Cadillacs, airplanes, or $150,000.00 homes. God will give them to you, but you have to get your priorities in order. He must be first place in your life.

Solomon Met The Conditions!

Solomon asked God for wisdom and knowledge. And here is what God said to him: ". . . Because this was in thine heart, and thou hast not asked riches, wealth, or honour, nor the life of thine enemies, neither yet hast asked long life; but hast asked wisdom and knowledge for thyself, that thou mayest judge my people, over whom I have made thee king: Wisdom and knowledge is granted unto thee; and I will give thee riches, and wealth, and honour, such as none of the kings have had that have been before thee, neither shall there any after thee have the like" (2 Chronicles 1:11, 12).

There are some wealthy people in the earth today. But they have not touched Solomon's wealth. He was so wealthy that when the people brought gifts to him (seeking his wisdom), they had to pile the silver up outside the gates. He received so many things that were more valuable than silver. He had heaps of silver! Solomon followed the instructions of his father, and those instructions were given to David by the inspiration of God.

Solomon met the conditions: he kept the law of the Lord; the statutes of God; and the commandments of God. And he prospered in whatever he did and wherever he went. Wisdom and knowledge were the things that produced that kind of prosperity in Solomon's life.

Without wisdom, understanding, and knowledge, prosperity is only a dream. Even though you achieve some degree of prosperity, without wisdom, knowledge, and understanding, you could lose it. Many people look at wealthy people and say, "Oh, they've got it made! They have more money than they know what to do with! They don't have a care in the world." Don't you believe it. Unless they are full of the wisdom of God, they are in trouble. Many wealthy people lack *Godly Wisdom for Prosperity*, and they are dying of diseases that medical science says are incurable. Their money cannot buy health. True prosperity covers more than just the things that money can buy.

The Bible says this about the man who finds wisdom: "Length of days is in her right hand; and in her left hand riches and honour" (Proverbs 3:16). If you follow the instructions — meet the conditions of God's Word, you will begin to prosper and live in health.

3
Seeking and Finding Wisdom

Wisdom is linked to prosperity. The Bible says, "Happy is the man who finds wisdom and gets understanding." Many people know only the worldly definition for *prosperity*. They miss out on what the Bible says about it. They have the idea that *prosperity* means just having a large bank account or more money than one needs. I want you to know that there are *many things that money cannot buy*. There have been a few times, not only in our personal lives but also in our ministry, when we needed something and we received it without making any kind of financial transaction (no money was involved). We got it with our faith.

The first airplane that the Lord gave to me was worth about $38,000 and I did not exchange one thin penny for it. God had spoken to some people to give it to me.

If prosperity consisted of having huge amounts of money only, then Aristotle Onassis would have probably been classified as one of the "most prosperous." Although he possessed great wealth (money), he could not buy his health, and he died of a disease that medical science said was incurable. I would not call that prosperity.

If you have a lot of money but you are dying, I do not believe that is God's definition of *prosperity*. The Bible says that if you will put the Word of God first place, and seek and find wisdom, it will not only give you riches and honor but also length of days. Good health is a part of God's plan for prosperity.

In the following Scripture passage you will find a complete definition of prosperity: "Happy is the man that findeth wisdom, and the man that getteth understanding. For the merchandise of it is better than the merchandise of silver, and the gain thereof than fine gold. She is more precious than rubies: and all the things thou canst desire are not to be compared unto her. Length of days is in her right hand; and in her left hand riches and honour. Her ways are ways of pleasantness, and all her paths are peace. She is a tree of life to them that lay hold upon her: and happy is every one that retaineth her. The Lord by wisdom hath founded the earth; by understanding hath he established the heavens. By his knowledge the depths are broken up, and the clouds drop down the dew. My son, let not them depart from thine eyes: keep sound wisdom and discretion: So shall they be life unto thy soul, and grace to thy neck. Then shalt thou walk in thy way safely, and thy foot shall not stumble. When thou liest down, thou shalt not be afraid: yea, thou shalt lie down, and thy sleep shall be sweet. Be not afraid of sudden fear, neither of the desolation of the wicked, when it cometh. For the Lord shall be thy confidence, and shall keep thy foot from being taken" (Proverbs 3:13-26).

God's definition of *prosperity* is not just having a lot of money. However, let's not exclude money; it is a part of the provision in the covenant of God. Riches and honor are a part of prosperity. Length of days is a part of it. Pleasantness and peace are a part of it. If you have a lot of money, but no peace, you do not have total prosperity. I am saying that *true biblical prosperity comes when you find the wisdom of God.* It includes all of these things. You will walk safely; your foot will not stumble. You will not be afraid when you lie down, and you will have sweet sleep. You will not turn and toss all night, worrying about your business, your wife or husband, or your children. Seeking and finding the wisdom of God will enable you to prosper to the point that you will have undisturbed sleep. You will not only be able to pay your bills, but you can help somebody else pay theirs. You will live in divine health, because you will know that you have become strong and established in the Word of God.

Total prosperity does not mean just being able to believe God for healing, yet you can't pay your bills. If you say, "Well, I don't have any problem believing for healing. But man! believing God for finances is something else." You still have to seek and find some more wisdom. In the sight of God, total prosperity not only will give you the ability to be blessed financially, but physically, mentally, spiritually, and socially. Praise God! That is part of the Abrahamic covenant. "And if you be Christ's, then are you heirs of the promise." The blessings of the Abrahamic covenant were not just spiritual blessings, not just mental blessings, and not just physical blessings. But God told him that he would be the head and not the tail; he would be above and not beneath, and all the nations of the earth would be afraid of them. That is social prosperity.

God's plan for prosperity for His children covers every area of their lives.

Wisdom And Knowledge Are Linked To Prosperity

You can get the wisdom of God concerning prosperity. Then, thank God, you won't have to fret or be concerned, or worried about prosperity. Prosperity is linked to wisdom.

Since Solomon became the most prosperous king, it only stands to reason that a man like that should have something to say about his wealth. One would think that God would give him a section in His Book to talk about what he did to get that way. And God did! He said, "Happy is the man that findeth wisdom and getteth understanding." We just read it!

The Key Word Is "Findeth"

"Happy is the man that findeth wisdom . . . ." That should automatically tell you that you are going to have to find something. Something is hidden. That something that is hidden is *wisdom*.

If I were to say to you, "Happy are you if you can find my car," that would automatically tell you that the car is hidden, and you must find it.

"Happy is the man that finds wisdom and the man that gets understanding." That tells me that *wisdom must be found first.* If something is hidden from you, you are going to have to work to find it. You will have to work to *find wisdom.*

You Cannot Live On Someone Else's Revelation

You must find wisdom yourself. I hope all the people who have tried to live by faith and said, "it didn't work" will read this book. It will work. It is because of lack of wisdom that it did not work for them. *They must find wisdom and get understanding.*

You cannot live on somebody else's revelation. It must be a revelation to you. I can tell you that God revealed to me: "Give, and it shall be given unto you; good measure, pressed down, and shaken together, and running over, shall men give into your bosom . . ." (Luke 6:38). And I can tell you how I applied that Scripture in my own life: how I gave to God, and how God has given back to me. BUT — if you go out and do something because I did it and not because of a revelation by the Spirit of God to your spirit, it probably won't work for you. IT HAS TO BE A REVELATION TO YOUR OWN HEART.

I will listen to inspiring testimonies. They motivate me. They tell me, "Bless God! If he can do it, I can. If he got his faith up to that level, I can get mine there too." But I do not just jump up and give away everything, and do everything that somebody else did, even though they got results. I let it become a revelation in my own heart. Once it becomes a revelation in my heart, nobody in town can stop me from doing it.

Every time I have approached it that way, it has worked. But when I tried to do it by somebody else's revelation, it hurt.

There were some men in the Bible who tried to live off of Paul's revelation. The apostle Paul came preaching in the name of Jesus, casting out devils, and ministering deliverance to the people. Some men saw him do it. They decided that if Paul could do it, they could. They got hold of a fellow who was demon-possessed, and they were going to cast the devil out of him. They said, "In the name of Jesus Christ, whom Paul preaches. . . ." And you know what happened! They lost their britches over it! Those demons jumped all over them, and tore their clothes off. They were trying to live by somebody else's revelation. (See Acts 19:13-16.)

I want you to know that I am giving you what the Spirit of God has revealed to me. You can take it, study it, keep notes, and meditate it until it becomes a revelation to you. You will have opened the door of your heart for the Holy Spirit to make it real to you. Now you are ready to act on it.

When you act on it, I will guarantee you, according to God's Word (James 1:20-22) it will work!

4
Finding Godly Wisdom Involves Work

"HAPPY IS THE MAN THAT FINDETH WISDOM, AND THE MAN THAT GETTETH UNDERSTANDING."

As I said in a previous chapter, *the faith walk is not a method of getting rich quickly.* It is not a three day or two-week experience. It is a way of life. If you are going to enjoy happiness, and all the other things that the Bible says that wisdom will produce, you are going to have to work at it. How? By acting on God's Word.

We read in Hebrews 4:11: *"Let us labour therefore to enter into that rest...."* You must work in order to rest.

Somebody said, "Now, I don't want to get caught up in works." I am not talking about religious works.

If wisdom is hidden it must be found. The next thing you must know is where it is hidden, and how you can find it. Proverbs 2:6 gives us a clue: "For the Lord giveth wisdom: out of his mouth cometh knowledge and understanding." *Out of His mouth!* OUT OF HIS MOUTH! OUT OF HIS MOUTH! When God talks, His wisdom is revealed. The Bible contains the wisdom that has come out of the mouth of God.

SOUND AND GODLY WISDOM IS HIDDEN *FOR* THE RIGHTEOUS; NOT *FROM THEM*.

You may say, "But I just can't get anything out of reading the Bible. It is too hard to understand."

No, it's not! Read verses six and seven together. "For the Lord giveth wisdom: out of his mouth cometh knowledge and understanding. He layeth up sound wisdom for the righteous: . . ." Can you see what God has hidden away for you? Let's read those same verses in the *Amplified Version of the Bible:* "For the Lord gives skillful and godly wisdom; from His mouth come knowledge and understanding. He hides away sound and godly Wisdom and stores it for the righteous . . . ." *Sound and godly wisdom is hidden for the righteous, not from them.*

New Testament Christians Have A Better Covenant

Somebody said, "Yes, but the Bible says that God's ways are past finding out. His thoughts are not our thoughts; they are higher than our thoughts."

YES! Yes! The Bible says that. But thank God, that is found in the Old Testament. Old Testament people were not born again, or baptized in the Holy Spirit of God, and they did not have the mind of Christ. The New Testament Christians can have all of this. If you are a Christian you are righteous (through the righteousness of Christ Jesus), and godly wisdom is hidden in God's Word for you.

You may ask, "Well, why is it hidden? I mean — after all — why didn't God make it easy, so we would not have to hunt for it?"

Because He doesn't want a group of lazy people. God wants an army. He hid sound and godly wisdom to your advantage, not disadvantage. God is not limiting us by hiding it. He is making us unlimited by hiding it FOR us, not FROM us. *Godly wisdom is hidden from satan.*

Since satan is the father of all unrighteousness, you can see that the wisdom of God is hidden from him, *from the unrighteous.* Satan has no access to the wisdom of God. The apostle Paul said in his letter to the Corinthians, "He that is spiritual judgeth all things, yet he himself is judged of no man" (1 Corinthians 2:15).

The Christian who is full of the wisdom of God looks strange to the world. They do not know what he is going to do next, or how he is going to act. They cannot understand it when somebody backs into his brand new automobile, and he doesn't stand up and curse or throw a fit, demanding somebody to pay. The world doesn't understand it when the man says, "I forgive you."

When the spiritual man is in lack, he gives. It hurts the devil when he has you "backed up against the wall" financially, and it looks as though he has you, and you can do nothing. Then you say, "Well, I only have five dollars left in my pocket, and I am going to give my way out of this."

The devil will yell, "You can't do that! It's too late."

You can say, "Yes, it is too late! It's too late for you, devil. I have given it and God will send my return."

The Bible says in Ephesians 3:10, "To the intent that now unto the principalities and powers in heavenly places might be known by the church the manifold wisdom of God." *God's wisdom has been made known to the church, and the principalities and powers cannot get in on it until the church tells them.*

The next time you ask God for wisdom, and you get it, don't go telling it to everybody you meet. That is when the devil finds out, and then he puts all those obstacles in front of you. Keep the devil guessing.

"X" Marks The Spot

If somebody gave you a treasure map, and told you to start at point "A", and you will find the treasure hidden where "X" marks the spot, you would follow all the clues. You would make the necessary arrangements to meet all the conditions. You know that the treasure is hidden at point "X", but that is not enough. Once you know where the treasure is buried, you must dig it out of there.

That treasure is the wisdom of God and it is hidden in God's Word. Get busy in the Word of God and dig it out. Begin to search the Word, speak the Word, and dwell on or meditate the Word. That word *meditate* means "to fix your mind on, or to dwell on."

In another sense, the word means *"to say over, and over, and over."*

You may say, "I don't have time to meditate on the Word of God." You have time to worry, don't you? *Worry is meditating or dwelling on what the devil says.* Worry fixes your mind on what has been said that is contrary to what God's Word says. If you have time to worry then you have time to find God's wisdom.

Godly Wisdom for Prosperity is found in the Word: "X" marks the spot. As you meditate the Word of God, you will open the door to the Spirit of God to reveal to you the understanding of His Word. "Happy is the man that getteth understanding."

5

The Need for Discipline

It is important to realize that you need to be balanced in the Word of God. This will take discipline. You should be established in the Word. As we talk about *Godly Wisdom for Prosperity*, we are going to be dealing with some things that are very touchy to some folks. You must read this very carefully, because there have been some words that have been loosely thrown around by some teachers that cause us to be hesitant to use those words, but they are scriptural. For example, it became very touchy for a while to use the word *submission*. The true meaning had become distorted. If the word *submission* was used, immediately the thought came, "Oh! they are one of them." *Submission* is a biblical word; it is scriptural. When it is applied scripturally, it will bring freedom, not bondage.

Another word that has been used loosely is the word *balance*. I want you to know that the word *balance* is not spelled C-O-M-P-R-O-M-I-S-E. However, many times when one talks about *balance*, that is the way it is spelled in the minds of some people. It is important that you know that you need to be balanced in the Word of God. You need to be established in the Word of God.

A lot of people go to the extreme. You should not do that. There is a group of people in the Body of Christ who believe that God wants His people to live in poverty. That is an extreme.

On the other hand, there is a group of people who found that God wants them to prosper, but they only have their eyes on money. That is an extreme.

There should be a balance between those two. There is a simple truth that is scriptural, and will produce happiness and joy, and blessings in your life. If you will learn what the Bible says about a balance for prosperity, it will not bind you; it will set you free.

It will not open the door for compromise, but it will put you in a position where you can get the pressure off. You will not become discouraged and defeated because it looks as though it is not working. It will keep you strong, and your goals and objectives will be intact. And — thank God! You will win.

You remember that God told Solomon that because he asked Him for wisdom and knowledge, He would also grant unto him riches, honour, and length of days. The reason that we are reading from the book of Proverbs is because Solomon is the author, and since God granted these things to him, it only stands to reason that we should learn from somebody who has been there. If we want to know something about prosperity, in whatever we do, and wherever we go, we should ask Solomon. Solomon walked in *Godly Wisdom for Prosperity*.

There is no need for you to ask poor old Brother Bill, who started out travelling for Jesus and lost everything he had. Why? Because he doesn't know anything. If he did, then he would not have lost everything.

You won't want to ask Sister Do-dad what she thinks about healing if she has been sick and weak her entire Christian life. If she knew that meditating the Word, doing the Word, and talking the Word brings prosperity, healing and success, she would not be a failure.

Some silly Christians will go out and ask other silly Christians, "What do you think about being filled with the Holy Ghost, and talking in tongues?"

And they will answer, *"Oh, those tongues are of the devil! Why, our church doesn't believe in tongues."* Why go ask somebody who doesn't talk in tongues what they think about them? If they knew anything, they would be doing it. SEEK OUT THE SUCCESSFUL ONES, NOT THE FAILURES.

Mr. A. W. Copeland (Kenneth Copeland's father) went into the insurance business at a late stage in his life. In a very short time, he became a regional manager in the state of Texas. He conducted meetings and seminars to train other men in how to become successful insurance salesmen. Because of wisdom, Mr. Copeland was a man of experience with a successful track record. He shared with the men everything that he had learned, and the things that worked for him. These are the words that Mr. Copeland shared with me. "You know, it is an amazing thing, I used to train men in how to be successful insurance salesmen. And you know, it beat anything I ever saw. Those men would go out and spend the day in the field, and not sell a policy. The next thing you know, you could find them down at the cafe sitting around a table with a bunch of 'do-nothings.' They would ask them, 'What do you think about selling insurance? Can you make a living selling insurance?'

"They would answer, 'No, we tried it. You can't make any money in it. That's the reason we are sitting here doing nothing.' "

They took the word of failures, rather than a successful person.

Christians will do the same thing. They will go around and talk to the people who have failed in their faith walk because of lack of wisdom. They will listen to them say, "Well, you know, we don't believe in that faith teaching in our church. Everybody who believed in that faith teaching, and stood on the Word, and confessed their healing, died. If God wants us to prosper He will prosper us. Why, after all, we have a businessman in our church right now who believed that faith teaching and lost everything he had." Don't listen to failures. They should have listened to what the successful persons said, gone to the Word of God and received the revelation in their spirit, and then acted upon it. The Word works!

Discipline Yourself To Spend Time In
The Word Of God

The Spirit of God once told me, "Son, the world will seek out a man with wisdom and understanding, who is successful. I will make that available to you if you will discipline yourself to spend your time in the Word."

That is a quest for me. I shall never be found guilty of not getting into the Word of God, and meditating the Word by day and by night. Meditating the Word is what got me "off my back." It is the thing that has prospered me.

I am still learning. There is so much more in God's Word that I have to learn. I am excited about what is available to me as the wisdom of God is imparted into my spirit, and I act upon it, and apply it to the circumstances of life.

There is no limitation to the man, woman, or child who will put the Word of God first place in their life.

Getting Wisdom And Understanding Takes Discipline

In the previous chapter you learned that the wisdom of God is hidden in His mouth. You also learned that it is not just going to fall on you. You are going to have to work to find it. The Bible says that, "Happy is the man that findeth wisdom, and the man that getteth understanding." To find something demands work.

Many times people just do not stop and think about it, but God would never make a statement about something being hidden if He did not also show us how it can be found and that one can attain it. They think that the Bible is telling them that there is something out there somewhere, but that they cannot have it, that He just wanted us to know that it is out there.

The Spirit of God does not do His people like that. Wisdom is hidden for the righteous man, and it can be found. Understanding can be found. That tells me, praise God, that we are going to have to get up off of our spiritual backsides and go to work.

Consider The Ant

There are laws of prosperity, and there are laws of poverty. Let's look at the following Scripture passage, and learn something from that little creature that steals your goodies on picnics. The ant has more wisdom than some Christians! "Go to the ant, thou sluggard; consider her ways, and be wise: Which having no guide, overseer, or ruler, Provideth her meat in the summer, and gathereth her food in the harvest. How long wilt thou sleep, O sluggard? when wilt thou arise out of thy sleep? Yet a little sleep, a little slumber, a little folding of the hands to sleep: So shall thy poverty come as one that travelleth, and thy want as an armed man." (Proverbs 6:6-11) There is a law that will produce poverty. All you have to do is sleep; become lazy. *A little sleep, a little slumber, a little folding of the hands, and I will guarantee you, poverty will come on you and overtake you.*

That tells me right there — if sleep, slumber, and spiritual laziness will produce poverty, then opposite actions will produce prosperity. The Christian who will meditate the Word by day and by night, is diligent and highly disciplined, will not be moved by circumstances, is not easily shaken, will continue to strive and press forward, thank God, prosperity will come on him and overtake him.

"Why doesn't He just prosper me anyway, without me having to do anything?"

He has already prospered you. The Bible says, "He has already obtained for us all things that pertain to life and godliness . . ." (See 2 Peter 1:3) But you are going to have to wake up, sluggard! Arise, and get it. IT TAKES DISCIPLINE.

6
Find — Get — Lay Hold — Retain

Finding wisdom is not necessarily physical work, but it is a job. It is work, seeking diligently the wisdom of God. You will find as you begin to study the Word and meditate the Word, you will spend hours upon hours of time just running the Scriptures through your consciousness. Working at it day after day, you will finally build a "flip-chart" in your heart. As you begin to meditate the Scriptures they will eventually become stored down in your spiritual computer, or heart (like on a flip-chart), and will pop up at the very moment you need them.

We talked about seeking wisdom in a previous chapter, but I will say again, as you meditate the Word of God you will find that the Lord gives wisdom. He hides sound wisdom for the righteous, not from them.

How do you find that wisdom? How does God release His wisdom? How does He make it available to His people?

The Bible tells us, "Out of his mouth cometh wisdom, knowledge, and understanding." You have His wisdom in printed form. *The Bible contains God's wisdom from cover to cover.*

How many Christians do you suppose there are who walk around with God's wisdom tucked under their arm, or on their coffee table, and don't even know it? I don't carry my Bible to impress people. I carry it in my heart to defeat the devil. Many Christians go around with God's wisdom already released out of His mouth (in their Bibles), but they do not get into the Word and meditate it. Then they cry, "I just don't understand it." Just owning a Bible does not guarantee you prosperity. *Until you take it out of the pages, and meditate it — fix your mind on it — and get it down into your spirit,* you will not find *Godly Wisdom for Prosperity.* It will be just another book to you.

Godly Wisdom Comes Through Spiritual Discernment

The natural mind cannot understand godly wisdom. It is foolishness to the natural mind. In order to understand this, you must — first of all, be born again — recreated. Then, *one of the most important things after being born of God is to be filled with the Spirit of God,* because the Spirit of God is the Revealer of the wisdom of God.

People who are not filled with the Holy Spirit are limited in how much revelation knowledge they can receive. Jesus said to His own disciples: ". . . It is expedient (more profitable) for you that I go away: for if I go not away, the Comforter will not come unto you" (John 16:7). He also said, "I have yet many things to say unto you, but ye cannot bear them now. Howbeit when he, the Spirit of truth, is come, he will guide you into all truth: for he shall not speak of himself; but whatsoever he shall hear, that shall he speak: and he will shew you things to come" (vv. 12, 13). Jesus is actually saying, "You are limited now because you are not filled with the mighty Holy Spirit of God — the Comforter — the Revealer of truth. And when I go away, I am going to send Him; He will not only be with you, but He will abide in you. Then when He abides in you, He will take everything that I wanted to say to you, and teach you."

"Happy is the man that *findeth* wisdom, and the man that *getteth* understanding. For the merchandise of it is better than the merchandise of silver, and the gain thereof than fine gold. She is more precious than rubies: and all the things thou canst desire are not to be compared unto her. Length of days is in her right hand; and in her left hand riches and honour" (Proverbs 3:13-16). Can you think of any two things that the world would rather have than prosperity and health? Men will do almost anything for success and health. He is telling us that when you allow wisdom to become the principal thing in your life, when you seek out godly wisdom, then along with that wisdom comes health, riches, and honor. "Her ways are ways of pleasantness, and all her paths are peace. She is a tree of life to them that *lay hold upon her:* and happy is every one that *retaineth* her" (vv. 17, 18).

I would like to emphasize some very important words concerning the above Scripture passage:

FINDETH; GETTETH; LAY HOLD UPON; RETAIN.

Three of those words are talking about something that you do before you find wisdom. The last word is something you do after you get it. Notice this: *find* wisdom; *get* understanding; *lay hold* upon her. Then — after you *find, get,* and *lay hold upon* — *retain.*

He put that in the Bible about retaining because there are a lot of Christians who have found out the wisdom of God, and prosperity was produced in their lives. Yet, when prosperity came to them, their priorities changed. They let wisdom go, and things, things, things became more important than the wisdom of God. *They did not retain wisdom.* Retaining is just as important as finding. In fact, I believe that retaining is more important than finding wisdom. What could be worse than going through life having wisdom and then losing it?

One of the major things that will cause one *not to retain the wisdom of God* is the allurement of things. When God's Word is injected into your life it will change unrighteousness to righteousness, sickness to health, and poverty to wealth. However, once you get hold of this principle and it begins to work in your life, it is easy to lose the wisdom of God that causes this to work. Sometimes it can be done unconsciously. You can get caught up in riches, after God has blessed you with a better home, a better automobile, and you are no longer struggling to just barely make ends meet. You are no longer under pressure or insecure. Then, it becomes easy to be less diligent than you once were when you were seeking and finding the wisdom of God.

Many Christians have this attitude: "Well, you know, I really spent a lot of time in the Word when I first heard this. I was in a jam then, when I was *seeking, finding* and *laying hold* on the Word of God. But I don't need that much Word now." Some of them will say, "Praise God! This principle got me out of that dump; put better clothes on my back, and money in the bank. I can get anything I want now."

Everything looks good to them (the lust of the flesh) and they see large neon signs saying, "Come and get me!" The next thing that happens is the allurement of things has become priority in their life, instead of the Word of God. This causes them to *not retain* the wisdom of God.

Never allow circumstances that are changed in your life, because of the wisdom of God, to cause you to stop seeking wisdom. This is not a principle to use until one need is met, and then forsake it until you are under pressure again.

God did not tell Joshua to meditate the Word by day and by night (Joshua 1:8) only when he had rivers to cross. Never lose sight of the importance of God's Word.

Do Not Forsake Wisdom

We read in Proverbs 4:1-10: "Hear, ye children, the instruction of a father, and attend to know understanding. For I give you good doctrine, forsake ye not my law. For I was my father's son, tender and only beloved in the sight of my mother. He taught me also, and said unto me, Let thine heart *retain my words: keep my commandments*, and live. *Get wisdom, get understanding: forget it not; neither decline from the words of my mouth. Forsake her not*, and she shall preserve thee: love her, and she shall keep thee. Wisdom is the principal thing; therefore *get wisdom:* and with all thy getting *get understanding*. Exalt her, and she shall promote thee: she shall bring thee to honour, when thou dost embrace her. She shall give to thine head an ornament of grace: a crown of glory shall she deliver to thee. Hear, O my son, and receive my sayings; and *the years of thy life shall be many*."

Evidently, you can forsake wisdom. You can *get it, have it, lay hold upon it, and then forsake it*. He tells us in the above Scripture passage to forsake her not. I believe that a lot of people have died prematurely simply because they did not lay hold upon the wisdom of God. "My son, attend to my words; incline thine ear unto my sayings. Let them not depart from thine eyes; keep them in the midst of thine heart. For they are life unto those that find them, and health to all their flesh." (vv. 20-22) Wisdom produces life.

We read in Proverbs 5:1, 2: "My son, attend unto my wisdom, and bow thine ear to my understanding: That thou mayest regard discretion, and that thy lips may keep knowledge." It is just as important to retain the wisdom of God as it is to find it.

FIND — GET — LAY HOLD — RETAIN GODLY WISDOM FOR PROSPERITY, LIFE AND HEALTH.

7
Guidelines for Prosperity

You are now on your way to find, get, lay hold upon, and retain *Godly Wisdom for Prosperity*. I shall now share with you something that I feel is very important which God shared with me. I simply call them *"Guidelines for Prosperity."*

NUMBER ONE: **GOD'S WORD IS THE GREATEST SOURCE .**

You must accept the fact that God's Word is the greatest source of wisdom, knowledge, and information on the subject of prosperity. There are all kinds of books that have been written on this subject. Until you know that God's Word is indeed the greatest source, and His Word is a revelation to you; it will not work for you as proficiently as it works for the other person who has obtained this revelation. As you read this book, you are reading what God revealed to me. What is better than this is to have God reveal it to you. He can reveal it to you as you read my book, but why get it secondhand when you can get it firsthand?

Of course, there are people who do not spend time in the Word for themselves. However, God wants to reach them so He will have us keep on writing books to be used as an aid in their study. *Books are aids and instruments to be used to awaken the Body of Christ to the wisdom of God.* I am not against reading books other than the Bible. I intend to write many of them. But I am saying this to you: Do not always depend upon somebody's book as your only means of acquiring revelation knowledge. Learn to get it from God's Word and the Holy Spirit. I read other people's books, and they inspire me. I always learn something; I always get new insight. But I am not waiting until someone writes another book to learn more about God and His plan for my life. I am not going to wait until Kenneth Copeland or his wife, Gloria, writes another book on *prosperity.* They may not get it out for a year or two, and I need to have deeper insight before that time. I am saying this to tell you that *God's Word is the greatest source of information on the subject of prosperity.* God will reveal it to you as you meditate His Word by day and by night. If you will make the decision to get in the Word and get that Word in your spirit, the Holy Spirit of God will accommodate you.

NUMBER TWO: **YOU MUST REALIZE THAT IT IS GOD'S WILL THAT YOU PROSPER.**

The second guideline for prosperity is basic. You must know that it is the will of God that you prosper. Until this fact becomes a reality in your life, you are limited. You must know without a shadow of a doubt that it is God's will that you prosper.

You may ask, "How in the world can I know that it is God's will that I prosper?"

Read the BOOK! It is expressed in His Word, not just one place, but many, praise God. Prosperity for

God's people is just as much a part of the substitutionary sacrifice of Jesus as His being made sin with your sin. Jesus not only died for your sin; He became sick with your sickness; He was made poor that you might be made rich. Know this — it is God's will that you prosper.

NUMBER THREE: PROSPERITY IS CONDITIONAL.

Since we talked about this in a previous chapter, you know that you must meet some conditions. Even though it is God's will that you prosper, it will not happen to you automatically. It is also the will of God that all men be saved and come into the knowledge of the truth, but everyone will not be saved because they will not meet the conditions. There is a condition to salvation: "That if thou shalt confess . . . ." If you do this, then you will be saved. Prosperity is the will of God. He has already made it available to you, and when you meet those conditions, He will back His Word. He will see to it that it is a reality in your life.

If you have this idea: "I know it is God's will that I prosper, and I know He will prosper me whenever He is ready," then you need to get back into the Word. He is ready! He is waiting on you. You must meet the conditions.

NUMBER FOUR: OBEDIENCE IS THE KEY.

If prosperity is conditional, then you must realize that *obedience is the key to prosperity*. You may say, "Oh, that is a word I don't like, Brother! I just do not like to obey."

Without obedience, you will not prosper.

Somebody said, "Yes, but that would be a sacrifice for me."

No! The Bible says that obedience is better than sacrifice. If you say that it would be a sacrifice to you, then do it in faith. When you obey in faith, God will honor it, then you will find that it will become easier to obey. I enjoy obeying God. I have new insight into it. Obeying puts me in the position of advantage, and it binds the devil. The Bible says, "If you are willing and obedient you shall eat the good of the land." (See Isaiah 1:19) I am willing to be obedient to the Lord.

A verse of Scripture that ties in with obedience is found in Job 36:11: "If they obey and serve him, they shall spend their days in prosperity, and their years in pleasures." Notice this condition: "IF." IF they what? "If they obey and serve him, they shall spend their days in prosperity, and their years in pleasure." Praise the Lord! It is good to be obedient.

NUMBER FIVE: **BE A GOOD STEWARD.**

When you see prosperity mentioned in the Bible it is always connected with *giving*. The Bible says that it is more blessed to give than to receive. (See Acts 20:35.) To the natural mind that is dumb, but not to the renewed mind. Make the decision to be a giver. You will never be able to out-give God.

I heard one preacher say, "Man! I'm in a terrible financial condition, but I am going to give my way out of this."

"Give and it shall be given unto you" is a cardinal law of God. God gave His only Son, and in return He got a whole family. He started it! Prosperity demands that you become a good steward. You should also realize the need for consistency in your giving.

Many Christians say, "Tithing doesn't work for me. I tried it, and I haven't received a return yet. The windows of heaven have not opened to me." It is consistency that causes that to work in your life. That is where *Godly Wisdom for Prosperity* comes in. Be consistent.

NUMBER SIX: **UNDERSTAND THAT PROSPERITY IS PROGRESSIVE**

Prosperity does not come on you all at one time. It is a progressive thing. Malachi 3:10 says, "Bring ye all the tithes into the storehouse, that there may be meat in mine house, and prove me now herewith, saith the Lord of hosts, if I will not open you the windows of heaven, and pour you out a blessing, that there shall not be room enough to receive it." This does not necessarily mean that it is going to happen to you all at once. But as you consistently tithe, then, progressively you are blessed to a degree or point in your life to where your consistency in tithing is going to open the windows of heaven unto you. Just as the blessings of Abraham, they will come on you and overtake you, progressively.

NUMBER SEVEN: **YOU MUST KNOW THE STUMBLING BLOCKS TO PROSPERITY**

Waste: You need to know the stumbling blocks to prosperity, and learn to avoid them. It is very easy when you have had nothing, and then have more than you need, to become wasteful. I didn't realize this at first, but Jesus taught on avoiding waste. He was not a penny-pincher, but do you remember when He fed the five thousand men, plus the women and children, on five loaves and two fishes? There were twelve baskets left over. What did He do with them? Jesus was a man who operated in the realm of abundance. However, He told the disciples to gather up the fragments that remained, *that nothing be lost.* He operated in abundance, but He did not waste anything. That tells me that waste can be a stumbling block to prosperity. (See Mark 6:34-44.)

Bad stewardship: Another stumbling block to prosperity is bad stewardship. I have talked to people who are believing God for prosperity, yet they do not take care of what they have. I shall be honest with you: until you learn to be a good steward over what you have, you are not ready for abundance.

My wife and I have believed God with our faith for everything that we own. God has given it to us. We stood on the authority of God's Word, and it is precious to us. Now — things do not cling to us. We will give it all away in a minute. In fact, I come home after being away in a meeting, and never know what my house is going to look like. My wife could give it all away while I am gone! We do not allow things to possess us.

When God gave me the first airplane, I put it in the hangar and as I stood there looking at it, suddenly the thought came to me: "What if God tells me to give it away tomorrow?"

Then the Spirit of God spoke to me. "Son, don't let anything that I bless you with possess you. If I instruct you to give it away, be willing to do it right now!"

I said, "Even before I get to fly it?"

"Even before you get to fly it," He said. "I am not trying to take anything away from you. If you are willing to give the shirt off your back, I am willing to bless you with the best. All I want you to be is willing."

I laid my hand on the nose of that airplane and said, "Father, in the name of Jesus of Nazareth, even though we have stood on the Word of God for two years for this piece of equipment, I'll give it tomorrow if that is what You desire. And I'll not think twice about it. In the name of Jesus, it's Yours, and I'll give it as You instruct me."

He said, "I appreciate that! Now enjoy it!" If God can trust you with little, He will make you ruler over much.

Bad stewardship has stopped a lot of people from prospering. A lot of them are believing God for a better automobile, and you can't even get in the one they are driving now for the junk that is piled up in it.

It is very easy sometimes when you begin to prosper to become loose with your prosperity. When you do, God has to fold His hands until you get back in line. He is very extravagant, but He will not waste.

I took my daughters to the store one afternoon to purchase a gift that they had picked out for their mother. When we got out of the automobile, we walked right in front of a western clothes shop. I very seldom get to *dress western* style, but when I do I love it. I had on my cowboy boots, my levis, and my western shirt. I only own about two pair of jeans and two western shirts, and one pair of boots because I wear a suit about ninety-five percent of the time. The Lord had just blessed me through someone giving me some money. I had it in my pocket at that time. I saw a big sign: "WESTERN JEANS 1/2 PRICE!" Oh! that looked good! I said, "Girls, you go on, I am going in here for a little while." I walked in there and decided that I just had to have those jeans. I didn't even try them on. I just picked up a pair that appeared to be my size, purchased them, and took them home when the girls finished shopping.

I hurried in to try on my new jeans, only to find that one leg was much longer than the other, and the zipper was sewn in crooked. To make matters much worse, printed right down on the bottom of the ticket were the words, "All sales final." That made me MAD!

Then, the Spirit of God said to me: "I want you to hang them in your closet where you can see them every time you go into your closet."

"Why?" I said.

"To remind you not to waste." Every time I walk into my closet to get out what I am going to wear, I see those stupid jeans that I can't even wear.

I said, "Thank you, Lord, in the name of Jesus! I am not a waster. I am faithful over little, and You are going to make me ruler over much."

Those jeans only cost $9.85, but I want you to know that in the past I have been just as stupid over something that cost $995. I keep those jeans right in front of me to remind me to use the wisdom of God, and discretion in everything that I do.

Prosperity is available to you. But you need to know about the stumbling blocks and learn how to avoid them. Stop wasting, and become a good steward over what you have. Be faithful over little, and God will make you ruler over much.

NUMBER EIGHT: **NEVER FORGET THAT GOD IS YOUR SOURCE**

Say: "God is my source. He meets all my needs according to His riches in glory, by Christ Jesus." God wants to be the "Provider" of all your needs. He is your Father and He loves you. Every good father wants the best for his children. "How much more shall your Heavenly Father give good gifts to those who love Him?"

8
Prosperity is Progressive

The Spirit of God reveals His wisdom to His people so that they can learn how to apply it in their affairs. Revelation knowledge comes to you so that you can apply it to your life. The Bible says that the man who is a doer of the Word shall be blessed in all his deeds. That is prosperity.

Meditation in the Word of God is the key to understanding God's wisdom. When that revealed knowledge has been given to you by the Spirit of God, you can observe to do it. You can act upon it and apply it to your life. Once you apply it, you have released a spiritual law and God will back it.

There has been a lot of teaching on prosperity, but I feel that many times we have failed to tell the people that it comes progressively. Many things have been left unsaid. Then when some Christians try to act on what they heard, many of them fail. They did not learn the conditions that had to be met before the spiritual laws of prosperity could work accurately.

I wish to emphasize this again: attaining prosperity in your life is progressive. Again, I want to say, it does not come on you all at once. There is some work to be done in the background. A good example of this principle is the making of a movie. The first time we went to California, we took our daughters to Universal Studios. We were amazed at the background work involved in creating a movie.

After we went back home we were watching one of those movies that we had seen them make back at Universal Studios. Some friends were watching with us, and we would tell them just how they did every thing in the background.

You see, we found out what was going on in the background. However, the only thing most moviegoers ever see is the finished product. The finished product (prosperity) is about all that some preachers and teachers have been guilty of presenting to the people. To be successful you must know all the steps that must be taken before you can attain prosperity.

God forbid that I only present the finished product. That is damaging to the Body of Christ. They could go to the Word and get it on their own. But there are a lot of *spiritual babies* out there, who will not get it for themselves. They have to be *bottle-fed first*. Many times you have to put the bottle in their mouth until they can learn how to hold it for themselves. Some of them even then will throw it up against the wall. But, I refuse to give up on them.

I am tired of the devil beating members of the Body of Christ. When a family comes into my office, who has been believing God for prosperity, and the devil has just absolutely run them around in circles, that makes me mad, not at them, but at the devil. I am out to hurt him, and the best way that I know how is by teaching them the Word.

You Are Going To Grow!

When I told God that I would pastor a church in Fort Worth, I believed that everybody in my congregation was going to prosper. I believed that they would live in divine health, and I told them, "I am not going to baby-sit with you. YOU are going to get on the Word, and you are going to grow. Now, I'll preach it to you, but we are not going to set up a nursery here."

Some people came in who lacked wisdom and understanding. I had to point out that without the wisdom of God, they could not have true prosperity. They had to learn that prosperity did not come to them overnight. It is progressive. They had to learn how to take it one step at a time.

However, there have been times when God just dumps one of those big ones on you. There are times when God's special manifestations of grace overtake you. But you do not live by special manifestations of grace. You must live by faith.

The Need For Wisdom

You should never lose sight of the need for wisdom. You need to learn all that you can about how to walk in wisdom. You should learn to walk step by step as you receive the revelation of God down into your spirit.

Deuteronomy 28 should be a familiar Scripture to you by now. The first verse is a most important one. "And it shall come to pass . . ." That tells me that something is going to come to pass. It will be progressive. "It shall come to pass, IF . . ." It did not say, "It shall come to pass regardless . . ." It said, "It shall come to pass, if . . ." There are some conditions to meet.

Somebody said, "Now wait a minute, Brother Savelle, this is the Old Testament. That has nothing to do with us!"

It doesn't? Then you may wish to tear the book of Galatians out of your Bible. Galatians 3:29 says, "And if ye be Christ's; then are ye Abraham's seed, and heirs according to the promise." How will you ever inherit the blessings if you don't go to the Old Testament and find out what they are?

"And it shall come to pass (progressive), if (condition) thou shalt hearken diligently (make a steady effort to accomplish) unto the voice of the Lord thy God, to observe and to do (meet the conditions) all his commandments which I command thee this day, that the Lord thy God will set thee on high above all nations of the earth." (Deuteronomy 28:1) That is *progressive*. He did not say anything about *instantly*. He said that all these blessings shall come to pass.

If all these blessings came on you all at one time, then you would just have to die and go on to heaven, because you could not be blessed any more for the rest of your life.

What About You?

Do you believe God's Word with all your heart? Have you made the decision that you are going to be obedient to the Word of God? Are you going to hearken diligently to His voice? If you have set that as a goal in your life, then the next verse will become a reality to you. "And all these blessings shall come on thee, and overtake thee, if thou shalt hearken unto the voice of the Lord thy God" (v. 2).

Now, I would like to ask you this. Since the time that you found out what God says in His Word about prosperity, hasn't it been better? Notice, prosperity began to come progressively.

I am in a much better condition today than that day back in 1969 when I discovered the truth in God's Word concerning prosperity. I have progressed. *And I'm not through yet!* I still have room for more!

You will remember Job 36:11: "If they obey and serve him, they shall spend their days in prosperity, and their years in pleasures." That tells you that prosperity is a progressive thing. It does not say, "year," singular; it says, "years," plural. In other words, you are going to progressively prosper every day of your life, IF you follow the instructions. And, finally, it will get to a point in your life that all of your days will be prosperous, and all of your years will be in pleasure. It will become a reality in your life that you are overtaken with blessings.

I am not overtaken yet, but I am on my way. I am confessing the Word of God that they are overtaking me. As I continue to live by the Word of God, there will come a point in my life when I will be completely overtaken with the blessings of God. I will just have to go dump some of them on you or someone else because I won't have room to contain them!

"And It Shall Come To Pass if . . . ."

Let's read it again. "And it shall come to pass, *if* thou shalt *hearken* diligently unto the voice of the Lord thy God, to observe and to *do* all his commandments which I command thee this day, that the Lord thy God will set thee on high above all nations of the earth: And all these blessings shall come on thee, and overtake thee, if thou shalt hearken unto the voice of the Lord thy God. Blessed shalt thou be in the city, and blessed shalt thou be in the field. Blessed shall be the fruit of thy body, and the fruit of thy ground, and the fruit of thy cattle, the increase of thy kine, and the flocks of thy sheep. Blessed shall be thy basket and thy store. Blessed shalt thou be when thou comest in, and blessed shalt thou be when thou goest out. The Lord shall cause thine enemies that rise up against thee to be smitten before thy face: they shall come out against thee one way, and flee before thee seven ways. The Lord shall command the blessing upon thee in thy storehouses, and in all that thou settest thine hand unto; and he shall bless thee in the land which the Lord thy God giveth thee. The Lord shall establish thee an holy people unto himself, as he hath sworn unto thee, if thou shalt keep the commandments of the Lord thy God, and walk in his ways. And all the people of the earth shall see that thou art called by the name of the Lord; and they shall be afraid of thee. And the Lord shall make thee plenteous in goods, in the fruit of thy body, and in the fruit of thy cattle, and in the fruit of thy ground, in the land which the Lord sware unto thy fathers to give thee. The Lord shall open unto thee his good treasure, the heaven to give the rain unto thy land in his season, and to bless all the work of thine hand: and thou shalt lend unto many nations, and thou shalt not borrow" (Deuteronomy 1:1-12). If the Lord is going to bless the work of your hand, it has to be a progressive thing. Everything that you set your hand to do: not just today, but tomorrow, and the next day, and the next day, and the next year, and the next decade, if you are still here. He is going to bless *all* the work of your hand, *progressively*.

PROSPERITY IS A PROGRESSIVE THING!

9

Borrowing Money—Is It Wrong?

The question that many Christians ask today is, "Is it wrong to borrow money?"

I am not advocating borrowing money, but I would like to share with you some important facts that are found in God's Word concerning this subject.

I will suggest that you consider what the Word says before you make your decision concerning borrowing money. We are told in Proverbs 22:7, "The rich ruleth over the poor, and the borrower is servant to the lender." God is not saying, "If you are having a problem getting your needs met or supplying food for your table, you had better not borrow money to do it." He wants you to operate on the level of your faith, not someone else's level. He wants you to know that there is a better way than always having to borrow. But you must start where you are and continue to develop your faith in His ability to supply your needs.

In the following Scripture verse, He is telling you that if you will do what He tells you to do — meet the conditions, there will come a time in your life when you will not need to borrow. You will be the lender. "The Lord shall open unto thee his good treasure, the heaven to give the rain unto thy land in his season, and to bless all the work of thine hand: and thou shalt lend unto many nations, and thou shalt not borrow" (Deuteronomy 28:12).

If it is a sin to borrow, then God is inviting you to help someone else to partake in sin. Because He said, ". . . thou shalt lend and not borrow." If you lend to someone then that makes him the borrower. Let's rightly divide the Word.

Set That Goal!

Being able to lend and not borrow is something that the believer can set as a goal. He can act on the Word of God concerning it, and it will come to pass in his life.

If you are in the position now that you have to live on borrowed money, then you can begin to live by God's Covenant and, PROGRESSIVELY, you will walk out of debt and never have to borrow again. You will be the lender to those who are in need.

You can even lend to God. Proverbs 19:17a says, "He that hath pity upon the poor lendeth unto the Lord. . . ." If the Lord sinning? He just borrowed from me, because I gave to the poor.

No! He doesn't like being in debt, so He added this to the above verse: ". . . and that which he hath given will he pay him again" (v. 17b).

You may be thinking, "Oh, hallelujah! I can hardly wait until Family Finance opens up tomorrow!"

Wait a minute! Before you run out and try to borrow money, remember: there is wisdom involved here. Please read this carefully: Good credit can be an asset to your financial success. However, God has a better plan. He says, "Owe no man anything but to love one another; for he that loveth another hath fulfilled the law" (Romans 13:8).

I dare say that almost every person who has read that Scripture verse was already in debt when he found it. I was so far in debt when I read that for the first time that I thought: "Oh, I wish I had found that when I was a child!" The day I found it, I realized that owing no man anything but love was going to be a progressive thing. I realized that I would have to begin to discipline myself where borrowing was concerned.

I want you to notice something else here. I am not trying to take Scriptures and pull them out of their place, to make them say what I want them to say. I am pointing out to you the wisdom that will keep you out of bondage. There are people who get under bondage because they misinterpret the Scriptures. This verse also reveals to us the need for believers to fulfill their financial obligations.

I ask you this: What is worse? Borrowing money, if that is the only avenue available to you, or destroying your Christian testimony by not fulfilling your financial obligations? I believe that God would be much more pleased with my keeping a strong witness to my creditor, than my not doing anything at all — hoping that he will forget that I owe him.

In the above Scripture passages, God is making it possible for you to set a goal for your life: an objective that can be obtained IF you will live by the Word of God.

A friend of mine, Happy Caldwell, once asked the Lord, "Lord, is it wrong to borrow?" The Lord said, "No, it is not wrong to borrow — it is wrong to be a borrower."

When Happy asked the Lord what a borrower was, the Lord asked him what a believer was. He said, "Well, a believer is somebody that believes, constantly; all the time; never stops; twenty-four hours a day; seven days a week."

The Lord said, "All right, put that into the realm of borrowing. A borrower is somebody who is always, constantly, continually borrowing. Everything from sugar to eggs, to shoes, to money." In other words, it is not wrong to borrow, but it is wrong to be a compulsive borrower. For some, this habit is difficult to break. They need to set a goal and learn how to say "no" to some things.

10

The Believer and Easy Credit

You should use wisdom before borrowing or buying on credit. It is not wrong to borrow, but many people do not know when to stop borrowing. They can easily get themselves into trouble where excessive borrowing is concerned.

Some people will stand up and declare: "It is wrong to have charge accounts. God wants you to pay cash for everything." The thing that is wrong is when you do not know how to use your charge account properly. It is wrong if you allow that charge account to control you. It is wrong when you allow your charge account to become an extension to your paycheck. Christians need to use wisdom and not get involved in extremes.

As we continue our study on finances and borrowing, let us read Deuteronomy 28:12b again: ". . . and thou shalt lend unto many nations, and thou shalt not borrow." In other words, if you will follow the instructions in the Word of God, there will *progressively* come a time in your life when you will be so blessed and so prosperous that you will not have to borrow. You will have more than enough for your own needs, and you will be able to lend to others.

PLEASE READ THIS CAREFULLY:

If you are in a situation where you need money desperately and your Word level is low, I ask you this: "What should you do? Is God interested in you having your needs met?" Of course He is.

Let's establish a point by looking into the realm of healing first. A lot of people believe that the faith message is a message against doctors. It is not. It is preaching against disease. It is preaching against satan, who is the author of disease. I would be wrong, and I would not be able to sleep at night if I preached a message that condemned anybody who goes to a doctor for help. God wants your body healed. If your faith level is low, you're having trouble believing what the Word says concerning healing, and it's difficult for you to let the Word sustain you — then I suggest that you go to the doctor, take the pill or prescription, get well and get into the Word. You can take a dose of God's medicine (Proverbs 4:22) at the same time you take the pill or prescription and get your Word level built up. Then, the next time you can let the Word sustain you instead of the medicine.

This holds true in the financial area too. If they (creditors) are threatening to come and repossess everything you have, and your Word level is low, you must get the pressure off as quickly as possible. If you must borrow to do it, then borrow. Then you should get into God's Word and never allow yourself to get into that type of situation again.

Keep A Good Christian Testimony

God wants your needs met. He does not want your Christian testimony destroyed. What kind of testimony can you have if they are carrying everything out of your house, and you have been witnessing to your neighbors? "Serve God. Trust God. He will meet all your needs."

Your neighbors may come over and ask, "What's happening?" You will have to answer, "Well, my creditors have come to get my furniture because I could not meet my obligations. I can't pay my notes!" Your neighbor will say, "Well, I thought God was your source. What happened?"

You cannot tell him that God missed it. There are no exceptions to the rule. God never misses it. His Word is true — it works. You are the one who missed it because of lack of knowledge. You possibly could have been acting presumptuously, thinking it was faith.

Somebody said, "Well! Why doesn't God just step in there and do something?" He has. He has given us His Word. He is faithful to honor His Word, not foolishness.

Many times a person does not listen closely enough when ministers are speaking on the subject of financial prosperity, and therefore they hear just enough to get into trouble. Some will even read this book and think, "Oh, hallelujah! now I can finally borrow, I must hurry up and finish reading before the bank closes." If you do this, then you need to read this book again. That kind of foolishness is what got you in the bad shape you are in, in the first place. Do not create unnecessary obligations that will burden you down with a sense of lack.

Somebody said, "Well, God is my source. I'll just go out and buy on credit everything I want and He will pay for it." You are going to be shocked. There are a lot of foolish Christians running around thinking, "God is my source. He meets all my needs, and now I can go get that Cadillac that I have been wanting all of my life." They run out and get that Cadillac along with a large monthly payment, and then they decide that they must have a Mark V to go with it, so they get that with another large monthly payment; and, of course, they think, "I've got to have a nice big home with a four car garage because I'm in the big times now." One thing leads to another, and all the time he is saying, "God is my source; God is my source." He has become so far in debt that he can't even buy food for dinner. He has created a burden of lack. That is not wisdom.

God still wants to be your source. He wants to meet your needs, but if you do like the person above, you have shoved God out. You should not take the fact that God is your source and twist it. It doesn't work that way. It only stands to reason, if you only have $200 a week coming in, you should not create a $400 a week expense. It will catch up with you somewhere.

Somebody said, "Yes, but God is my source. He will bring me the other $200." Do you truly believe that or are you hoping He will do it? If not, then that's not faith, it's foolishness. A lot of people overextend themselves and it puts limitations on them. Neither their faith, nor their Word level can sustain that kind of expense.

It Is A Progressive Thing

When we started out in our ministry, we had enough cash for what it was going to take to operate for one week. We steadily progressed. As the ministry grew, it took more money. Now it takes more money to operate it for one week than it took to operate for a month when we first started. I am saying that it just continually progresses. Every time my faith grows the needs grow right along with it. The worst thing I could do is double my expenses tomorrow, just because the Word says that God is my source. My faith is at the level to sustain what I am doing right now, not what I am going to do next year. I have a year to get my faith increased before I walk into what I shall be doing next year.

It may take $50,000 a day next year to keep the doors open, I do not know; but I can guarantee you my faith is not ready for next year. My faith can sustain what I am doing right now; next month it will be a different story; next year is a different story. The most valuable thing for me to understand is this: *I am not going to be able to sustain or be sustained if my expenses increase and my Word level decreases.*

When things get better, you should not begin to slack off of the Word. You should meditate the Word day and night. Don't create a lot of expenses that will put on you a burden of lack. Simply ask yourself, "Is this going to put a strain on me and my budget?" If it does, don't hurry into it. Just hold off and go feed your faith. Increase your Word level until you ask yourself that question and you can say, "No, in the name of Jesus, my faith is capable of producing this." When there is no hesitation in your spirit, then you are ready.

I have read many articles concerning this subject. Most economists suggest: "Ask yourself, do you really need the thing that you are planning to go in debt for."

Did you know that a large percentage of American couples today are facing bankruptcy? That is staggering. I'm not just talking about young married people, that includes all married people regardless of age. One of the reasons for this problem is that credit is so easy to get and people overextend themselves.

Right across the street from my Evangelistic offices is a used car lot. They have a big sign up there that says, "We tote the note. No credit check needed." All you have to do is walk in there and pay $50.00 down and $5.00 a week. Do not think that they are doing you a favor. They are profiting by giving you easy credit: no credit check and no questions asked — they are going to come out ahead, somehow.

It is easy to overextend yourself and plunge into indebtedness. Once this happens, it will take a lot of discipline on your part to overcome this problem.

Pay Tribute To Whom Tribute Is Due

The Holy Spirit inspired Paul to write the following Scripture passage, "Let every soul be subject unto the higher powers. For there is no power but of God: the powers that be are ordained of God. Whosoever therefore resisteth the power, resisteth the ordinance of God: and they that resist shall receive to themselves damnation. For rulers are not a terror to good works, but to the evil. Wilt thou then not be afraid of the power? do that which is good, and thou shalt have praise of the same: For he is the minister of God to thee for good. But if thou do that which is evil, be afraid; for he beareth not the sword in vain: for he is the minister of God, a revenger to execute wrath upon him that doeth evil. Wherefore ye must needs be subject, not only for wrath, but for conscience sake. For this cause pay ye tribute also: for they are God's ministers, attending continually upon this very thing. Render therefore to all their dues: tribute to whom tribute is due; custom to whom custom; fear to whom fear; honour to whom honour. Owe no man any thing, but to love one another: for he that loveth another hath fulfilled the law" (Romans 13:1-8).

As you read all of the above Scripture passage, you can see that it is not talking about money only. Verse 7 said, "Render therefore to all their dues, tribute to whom tribute is due . . ." That includes all obligations. He is telling us to fulfill every obligation; pay your bills properly; handle every affair with discretion and good judgment. Don't allow your obligations to go unattended. If honour is due then give it, if money is due then pay it, and if reverence or respect is due then express it — OWE NO MAN ANYTHING, BUT LOVE!

Paul is telling you to pay tribute to whom tribute is due. In other words, "Be a good business-minded person." If you are honest and a good business-minded person, you have and will use discretion; you will operate wisely in your financial affairs and after you pay tribute to whom it is due, you will owe that person nothing except to love him.

Let's suppose you buy a car, pay $500 down, finance the rest of it for $169.52 per month for the next 36 months. When it comes time for you to pay on the note — pay it. Regardless of whether the old car runs or falls apart after you bought it, and you don't like it; you are still obligated to pay the note.

Paul did not say, "Do not borrow money." He did not say, "Do not finance a car," and he did not say, "Do not have a mortgage on your home." He did say, *"Pay tribute to whom tribute is due . . ."* It is possible that at this exact moment your faith is not at the level that you could buy a new home without borrowing the money. God does not want you living out in the street. Your faith level may not be at the point where you can pay cash for an automobile. An automobile is a "must" these days, and God wants you to have one, but He does want you to use wisdom here. As you progressively operate in the covenant of Jesus Christ in your life, there will come a time when you will not have to go to a *savings and loan company* for a mortgage to buy a home or an automobile. You will be able to pay cash.

When you overextend yourself is when you get into trouble, because then you cannot pay tribute to whom tribute is due. Learn to handle your financial affairs with wisdom and discretion.

11
The Christian and Credit Cards

Some people think that the use of credit cards is a sin for Christians. Others think that everybody should have at least ten. Some use their charge cards as an extension to their paychecks. They may only make $200 each week but think, "Yes, but I have five charge cards." That is not wisdom. The wisdom comes when the Christian has the ability to say, "No, I'll not use my charge card for unnecessary items."

Credit Cards Can Be Useful

We operate in a ministry that takes us throughout the United States almost every week. When we first started this ministry, it was very small. There was only myself, my wife Carolyn and one secretary. At that time the office rent was low, and a secretary's wage was not nearly as high as it is now. People were just finding out about our ministry and there was a minimum expense involved as we began to travel all over the country. I could carry enough cash in my pocket to pay all the bills.

God blessed our ministry and it kept growing. At the present time there are five or six people who travel with us, sometimes there will be as many as ten or twelve. We usually have a vehicle on the road, and an airplane. There are motel rooms and rent to pay on the auditoriums; that calls for a lot of money. I cannot carry the amount of money around that is needed to meet the expenses of the meetings. It is not uncommon for one meeting to cost $10,000 to $15,000 just in expenses alone. Carrying $15,000 in cash around in my pocket is not wisdom.

Somebody said, "But the angel of the Lord encamps around about those that fear Him." Yes! and they are probably the same people that argue about if it's faith to lock your car doors. What they don't realize is that they are providing open doors for satan. I know what I will do, it's others that I'm not too sure of. They could also go out and sleep in the streets of Harlem tonight, but that doesn't prove that they have great faith.

As the ministry continued to grow, the wiser thing for me to do was obtain some useful credit cards. I formerly carried my check book, but most hotels have stopped accepting personal checks as well as company checks. I now use gasoline credit cards to purchase gasoline, plus major credit cards for our motel expenses. My point is this: credit cards can be used to your advantage if you use wisdom, but you can get into trouble when you overextend the use of credit cards. The wisdom is in using the credit card to your benefit, and not to your destruction.

The Apostle Paul Had A Charge Account!

Somebody said, "I just do not believe in having charge accounts. The Bible says, 'owe no man anything but to love him.' " That's fine, I'm not advocating having credit cards. However, don't try to put others in bondage by telling them that it is a sin to have them.

Paul had a charge account. He is also the one who was inspired by the Holy Spirit to say, "Owe no man anything but to love one another . . ." Paul also wrote this letter to Philemon: "I beseech thee for my son Onesimus, whom I have begotten in my bonds: Which in time past was to thee unprofitable, but now profitable to thee and to me: Whom I have sent again: thou therefore receive him, that is, mine own bowels: Whom I would have retained with me, that in thy stead he might have ministered unto me in the bonds of the gospel: But without thy mind would I do nothing; that thy benefit should not be as it were of necessity, but willingly. For perhaps he therefore departed for a season, that thou shouldest receive him for ever; Not now as a servant, but above a servant, a brother beloved, specially to me, but how much more unto thee, both in the flesh, and in the Lord? If thou count me therefore a partner, receive him as myself. If he hath wronged thee, or oweth thee ought, PUT THAT ON MINE ACCOUNT; I Paul have written it with mine own hand, I will repay it . . ." (Philemon 10-19)

Paul used wisdom along with his charge account. He could have written to Philemon about every person who went through town, "Take care of him and put it on my charge account . . . ," until he overextended himself and his account. That would have destroyed him. Paul said, "I will repay thee . . . ."

Living by the New Testament will put you in a position where you will eventually owe no man anything but to love him. When you seek and find Godly Wisdom it will exalt you and cause the blessings of God to come on you and overtake you to the point that you will not have to borrow. You will have more than enough; not only for yourself, but many others.

12

Get the Pressure Off and Your Word Level Up

If you do not have food on the table for your family, and you haven't been able to meet your bills in months, you are under pressure. You must do what is necessary to get the pressure off. I can tell you this: if there has been no manifestation of your needs being met, if you are under pressure and you have not been in the Word, you have nothing working for you.

If this is the case, my suggestion is this: Do whatever is necessary to get the pressure off. Then get back into the Word of God and feed your spirit. As you become strong in the Word, you do not have to allow yourself to get into that kind of situation again.

God Will Meet You At The Level Of Your Faith

An example of this is found in 2 Kings 4:1-7. We read in verses 1-3, "Now there cried a certain woman of the wives of the sons of the prophets unto Elisha, saying, Thy servant, my husband is dead; and thou knowest that thy servant did fear the Lord: and the creditor is come to take unto him my two sons to be bondsmen . . ." Notice, the woman was under serious pressure. She was deeply in debt, and the creditor was going to take her sons if she didn't pay the debt. She could do nothing for herself. Her faith level was low, and she had to seek the aid of somebody else. She went to Elisha, a prophet of God (God's mouthpiece), "And Elisha said unto her, What shall I do for thee? tell me, what hast thou in the house? And she said, Thine handmaid hath not anything in the house, save a pot of oil. Then he said, Go, borrow thee vessels abroad of all thy neighbours, even empty vessels; borrow not a few."

The prophet of God had instructed her to do those things that were necessary to get the pressure off. "Go, borrow some vessels. Don't borrow a few. Borrow many vessels." And he said to her, "Take the two boys with you, and lock yourselves in your house. Take the one vessel of oil that you have, and pour it into all those borrowed vessels. The oil will multiply. It will fill every vessel. Then you can take all of that oil and sell it, and pay your debt, and you and your boys can live on what you have left over" (Author's paraphrase).

The woman had to use her level of faith, and God took the pressure off. Elisha had to get down on her level, and that was the place where she could follow his instructions. She could go borrow many empty vessels, lock herself and her sons in the house and pour the oil from one vessel to the other. God met her there; she met the conditions and God honored it. He brought her out of debt, and she even had enough for herself and her boys to live on.

Poverty Is A Curse Of The Law

Being beneath and not above is a curse, but the Bible tells us in the book of Galatians that *Christ redeemed us from the curse of the law.* When most of us found that out, we were already beneath and not above. Some of us were the tail and not the head; however, we knew that we did not have to remain in that situation. Jesus took care of that situation for us nearly 2,000 years ago. This gives us something to set as a goal for our lives.

On February 11, 1969, at about 3:00 a.m. I accepted Jesus Christ of Nazareth as the Lord of my life. When He became my Lord my nature changed, I was reborn, but my check book did not change. Of course, God could have immediately sent somebody to pay all of my bills the moment I accepted Him as Lord, but in my case He didn't work that way. In fact, I have not heard of any cases where somebody got born again; completely healed; out of debt; had no more negative thoughts and every circumstance in their lives changed all at once. Total prosperity is a progressive thing. It depends upon what you do with God's Word. The expression of God's will hung on the cross nearly 2,000 years ago. God wants you out from under the curse. It is ridiculous for someone to say that God loves poverty. In God's sight poverty is a curse, not a blessing. He expressed what He thought about poverty when He redeemed us from the curse of the law.

That does not mean that we will automatically get out of debt. But as we follow the instructions of God's Word and become obedient to His Word, then that covenant principle can become a reality in our lives.

We will begin to walk out of the old way of living and into a new way of life.

Make the Word of God first place in your life and you will prosper in whatever you do and wherever you go.

13
Beware of Deception

Several years ago when my wife and I started learning the faith message we were living in Shreveport, Louisiana. I had become acquainted with Brother Kenneth Copeland. I learned that he was coming to Shreveport to conduct a seminar, and I wanted to see him and talk with him because I had at least 900 questions to ask him.

On the way to Shreveport, Brother Copeland and his family experienced an automobile accident. Brother Copeland knew that I was an automotive paint and body man prior to entering the ministry. When he got into Shreveport, he contacted me to see if I could repair his automobile while he was conducting the seminar.

I had all of those questions that I wanted to unload on him; but I had learned enough from seeing him in meetings and listening to his tapes, that I knew I probably would not have an opportunity to talk to him.

I said, "Now, God, I have all these questions, and right now I do not know anybody who has the answers except Brother Copeland. I want to talk to him, *but I'm not going to push myself on him; I'm not going to corner him, and I'm not going to trap him.* If he is the avenue that You are going to use to get those answers to me — until I learn how to get them from You myself, then You will just have to get him to start the conversation, because I'll not open my mouth." There he stood, and there I was working on his car, with all those questions on the inside of me.

Brother Copeland started asking me questions about what I was doing to his car, and I would answer him. Finally, I had to stand up and stop what I was doing in order to talk to him. He started talking about some things in the Word and that just kept leading into something else. Eventually, it opened the door for me to ask my questions.

I said, "Brother Copeland, I have never heard anything like what you preach. I know in my heart that it is right, but I want to ask you one thing . . . I'm not having any problem believing God for healing. When I found the Scriptures that said I was healed, I never had another problem with that. The moment I read Matthew 8:17, Isaiah 53:5, and 1 Peter 2:24, I never doubted that it was the will of God to heal me . . . ." But the question of financial prosperity was another thing. Finances were eating me up. I just could not understand how God could prosper me, and the devil was trying his best to destroy me over it. I was about twenty-one years old, and several thousand dollars in debt. I could not get the Word to work in that area and I was in trouble. My credit was so bad, and I was so far behind, that I had no place to go. The Word of God had to work for me or I was finished.

There was nothing left for Jerry Savelle to do except just go on and fail.

I asked him, "How do you get God to meet your needs financially?" Brother Copeland said, "Well, Jerry, it's not a matter of getting God to do something, because He has already done all He is going to do about your finances."

I said, "He has? Do you mean that He is going to leave me in this shape? This is all He is going to do?" "No!" he said, "He has already done all that was necessary at Calvary." Then he said, "Jerry, don't you know that the shadow of a dog never bit anybody?"

I thought, "Bless his heart! Poor thing! He has been standing out here in the sun too long, and breathing this paint thinner has gone to his head."

He stood there and looked at me with those piercing eyes as he said, "The shadow of a dog never bit anybody."

I thought, "That is the big answer that I have been looking for all these months? What in the world has the shadow of a dog not biting anybody have to do with my financial condition?"

He said, "Jerry, the devil cannot defeat you financially; and he will not defeat you financially. If he could he would have already done it before he let you get this far." He asked me, "When you confessed that Jesus is Lord, and you believed in your heart that God raised Him from the dead, did you notice that there was absolutely nothing that hell could do to keep you from being born again? Satan had to stand there and watch God recreate you. He was absolutely helpless, and could not stop it. That decision that you made when you were born again is the same kind of decision that you have to make to be prosperous. When you make that decision, and will base your life on it, the devil is helpless. He will have to stand by and watch it happen." He said again, "If the devil could have beaten you he would have already done it before he let you get this far, because the more Word you get into you the more dangerous you are going to become to him. The devil is trying to get you to fall for the symptoms of lack. How many dogs' shadows have you ever known to hurt someone? Not a one. But you can walk down the street and if you see the shadow of a dog on a building, many times that very shadow will frighten you . . . . the dog doesn't even have to bite . . . . all you have to do is see his shadow."

"How many people in New York City do you suppose have been robbed by what appeared to be a gun? How many banks do you suppose have yielded $50,000 or more over to a guy with a toy pistol? See what I am saying? DECEPTION. The devil has been trying to get you to fall for the symptoms of lack, to get you to fall for the shadows. The shadow cannot hurt you, but if you yield to it, the deception that satan is using will destroy you." He said, "Jerry, when you realize that the devil cannot defeat you financially, anymore than he can defeat you where your salvation is concerned, then you are going to be a winner!"

I'll tell you, that just set me free, right then! Praise God! Since that time, if a crisis arises I think about the shadow of a dog never biting anybody. That is a symptom, and the symptom cannot defeat me unless I allow it to deceive me into yielding and giving up. I'll not fall for the devil's deception.

Christ has redeemed us from the curse of the law; and, thank God, He has made us the recipients of the blessings of Abraham. The blessings of Abraham actually belong to us. If you meet the conditions there is nothing that satan can do to stop that Word from coming to pass. The only thing that he can do that will work — if you allow him — is to deceive you. When the conditions are met satan is finished; no weapon formed against you will prosper.

The apostle Paul put it this way: "We are not ignorant of satan's devices, lest he get the advantage over us" (See 2 Corinthians 2:11). I know exactly how that rat plays. He does not play fair; he is a deceiver, and I have learned how to spot him. I am not ignorant of his method of operation. I have seen him at work, and I refuse to be deceived. When you know how he operates, the methods that he uses and you realize that *his number one weapon is deception*, then you are in the position of advantage.

Stay In The Game

The Lord once told me this: "Son, when the symptoms become greater and when it looks like the pressure is more severe, that should be a good indication to you that satan has just fired his best shot; and if that doesn't knock you over, he is finished and you can walk right over him."

When the greatest pressure comes on you, don't give up. Stand your ground! A lot of Christians will give up. All satan has to do is throw a little dart and they will run. Learn to fight a good fight. A good fight is when you win.

I like what Buddy Harrison once said, "Just because you fail it's not over, praise God. Don't allow that failure to stop you." Get up, brush yourself off, and ask God to forgive you for missing the mark. Get back on the Word of God.

The promises are ours. Let's read them: *"And it shall come to pass, if thou shalt hearken diligently unto the voice of the Lord thy God, to observe and to do all his commandments which I command thee this day, that the Lord thy God will set thee on high above all nations of the earth:*

"And all these blessings shall come on thee, and overtake thee, if thou shalt hearken unto the voice of the Lord thy God.

"Blessed shalt thou be in the city, and blessed shall thou be in the field.

"Blessed shall be the fruit of thy body, and the fruit of thy ground, and the fruit of thy cattle, the increase of thy kine, and the flocks of thy sheep.

"Blessed shall be thy basket and thy store.

"Blessed shalt thou be when thou comest in, and blessed shalt thou be when thou goest out.

"The Lord shall cause thine enemies that rise up against thee to be smitten before thy face: they shall

come out against thee one way, and flee before thee seven ways.

"The Lord shall command the blessing upon thee in thy storehouses, and in all that thou settest thine hand unto; and he shall bless thee in the land which the Lord thy God giveth thee.

"The Lord shall establish thee an holy people unto himself, as he hath sworn unto thee, if thou shalt keep the commandments of the Lord thy God, and walk in his ways.

"And all people of the earth shall see that thou art called by the name of the Lord; and they shall be afraid of thee.

"And the Lord shall make thee plenteous in goods, in the fruit of thy body, and in the fruit of thy cattle, and in the fruit of thy ground, in the land which the Lord sware unto thy fathers to give thee.

"The Lord shall open unto thee his good treasure, the heaven to give the rain unto thy land in his season, and to bless all the work of thine hand: and thou shalt lend unto many nations, and thou shalt not borrow.

"And the Lord shall make thee the head, and not the tail; and thou shalt be above only, and thou shalt not be beneath; if that thou hearken unto the commandments of the Lord thy God, which I command thee this day, to observe and to do them:

"And thou shalt not go aside from any of the words which I command thee this day, to the right hand, or to the left, to go after other gods to serve them" (Deuteronomy 28:1-14).

There, you have the promises or the blessings of Abraham. And, if you belong to Christ then you are an heir of the promise. I want you to know that you have a right to be blessed; to be set upon high; to be overtaken by blessings; to be in a position where you shall lend and not borrow, and where you will be plenteous in good things.

God is not against you having things. He is against things having you.

You don't have to wait until you get to heaven to enjoy a prosperous life. Deuteronomy 28 is not talking about how you are going to live when you get to heaven. This is what you can have while you live here on the earth. If you will get a picture of that on the inside of you it will become a motivating thing. You will refuse to allow any obstacle to get in your way, because you are determined to live the way that God said that you could.

14
Follow God's Instructions

The life of faith is a life that demands diligence. You cannot be slothful. When I first started in the ministry the Spirit of God said to me, "In your preparation for the ministry I am going to require of you not less than eight hours a day in the Word." Those were *my* instructions. God told *me* to do that. I'm not saying that is what you should do, unless the Spirit of God specifically tells you to do it. That doesn't mean that everybody should quit their jobs and spend eight hours a day in the Word. NO! Many people have tried that without God telling them to do it by His Spirit, and they failed. I was being prepared for the ministry. And He said, "I want you to treat it like your job." Then He said, "Son, if you don't follow My instructions then do not expect to be paid."

When I was working as an automotive body man, I worked on commission. If I did not go to the shop, I didn't draw a check on Friday. If I went to the shop and just sat in my stall and did not work, I didn't draw a check. If I worked I drew a commission, and the faster I worked the more jobs I completed and the more money I made.

It was the same when I went to work for the Lord. If I did not do what was required of me, then I could not expect to have my needs met. Living by faith does not mean, "Thou shalt not work." It just simply means confidence in God's Word and its authority alone.

You Must Get Into God's Word

You will fail if you just sit in your bedroom or living room and watch television and never spend time in the Word.

The Bible doesn't say, "Faith cometh by watching General Hospital." Faith comes by hearing, and hearing by the Word of God. *It is what you do with God's Word that causes you to be blessed.*

You will remember that David told Solomon in 1 Kings 2:1-3, "You will prosper in whatever you do, and wherever you go, IF you keep the charge of the Lord thy God; walk in his ways; keep his statutes and his commandments; his judgments, and his testimonies." Jesus put it this way: "If you abide in me, and my words abide in you, you shall ask what you will, and it shall be done unto you" (John 15:7; Author's paraphrase). James 1:20-23 says, "Be ye not hearers of the Word only, but doers" (Author's paraphrase). Those are some of the conditions that you must meet. Joshua 1:6-9, says, "Be strong and of a good courage: for unto this people shalt thou divide for an inheritance the land, which I sware unto their fathers to give them. Only be thou strong and very courageous, that thou mayest observe to do according to all the law, which Moses my servant commanded thee: turn not from it to the right hand or to the left, that thou mayest prosper whithersoever thou goest. This book of the law shall not depart out of thy mouth; but thou shalt meditate therein day and night, that thou mayest observe to do according to all that is written therein: for then thou shalt make thy way prosperous, and then thou shalt have good success."

You can see by the above Scripture passage that talking the Word, meditating the Word, and acting on the Word are the conditions for prosperity and success. "Have not I commanded thee? Be strong and of a good courage; be not afraid, neither be thou dismayed: for the Lord thy God is with thee whithersoever thou goest." He is saying, "Be free from fear; do not be dismayed; do not become discouraged. Don't give up!" Those, also, are conditions for prosperity and success.

Obedience Is The Key

David is talking to Solomon again in 1 Chronicles 22:10-13: "He shall build an house for my name; and he shall be my son, and I will be his father; and I will establish the throne of his kingdom over Israel for ever. Now, my son, the Lord be with thee; and prosper thou, and build the house of the Lord thy God, as he hath said of thee. Only the Lord give thee wisdom and understanding, and give thee charge concerning Israel, that thou mayest keep the law of the Lord thy God. Then shalt thou prosper, if thou takest heed to fulfil the statutes and judgments which the Lord charged Moses with concerning Israel: be strong, and of good courage; dread not, nor be dismayed."

When you have wisdom and understanding, you will prosper. Can you see what he is saying here? Be strong, be of good courage, dread not, nor be dismayed, get wisdom and understanding. Talk the Word; meditate the Word; act on the Word; and walk in the Word. The results are prosperity, success and blessings will overtake you. You will be the head and not the tail, above and not beneath. This is the fulfillment of God's Word in your life when the conditions are met.

Prosperity Is Available To Everyone

If you will read 2 Chronicles 26, you will read about one of the most prosperous kings that Israel ever had. King Uzziah was only sixteen years of age. It says in verses 4, 5, "And he did that which was right in the sight of the Lord, according to all that his father Amaziah did. And he sought God in the days of Zechariah, who had understanding in the visions of God: and as long as he sought the Lord, God made him to prosper." NOTE: "As long as he sought the Lord, God made him to prosper."

If you continue reading you will find that there came a time in this man's life when he was so prosperous that he did like a lot of other people do. Verse 16 says, "But when he was strong, his heart was lifted up to his destruction: for he transgressed against the Lord his God, and went into the temple of the Lord to burn incense upon the altar of incense." There is a danger in the deceitfulness of riches.

Jesus listed the deceitfulness of riches as one of the five major avenues that satan uses to steal the Word from us (Mark 4:14-18). He said affliction, persecution, the cares of this world, the lust of other things, and the deceitfulness of riches will steal God's Word from your heart. Many people cannot handle prosperity. If they begin to prosper, it goes to their heads. Their hearts get lifted up and filled with pride. They no longer acknowledge God as their source.

When God has blessed, they will say, "I did this and I did that." Then pride will cause their hearts to be lifted up, and they will transgress against God. It takes the wisdom of God to prosper, and it also takes the wisdom of God to maintain that prosperity.

The Word says, "If they obey and serve him, they shall spend their days in prosperity and their years in pleasures" (Job 36:11).

I would like to point out three things that we have discovered.

FIRST: *It is without doubt that it is the will of God that we prosper.*

SECOND: *By now, you must know prosperity is conditional.*

THIRD: *The Scriptures that we have been studying also reveal to us that obedience is the key to prosperity.*

If you are going to prosper and have good success, you must talk the Word, meditate the Word, and act on the Word.

15
Be One of The Rare Kind

As you begin to prosper, it is important that you never forget Who is your source. "Beware that thou forget not the Lord thy God, in not keeping his commandments, and his judgments, and his statutes, which I command thee this day: Lest when thou hast eaten and art full, and hast built goodly houses, and dwelt therein; And when thy herds and thy flocks multiply, and thy silver and thy gold is multiplied, and all that thou hast is multiplied; Then thine heart be lifted up, and thou forget the Lord thy God, which brought thee forth out of the land of Egypt, from the house of bondage; Who led thee through that great and terrible wilderness, wherein were fiery serpents, and scorpions, and drought, where there was no water; who brought thee forth water out of the rock of flint; Who fed thee in the wilderness with manna, which thy fathers knew not, that he might humble thee, and that he might prove thee, to do thee good at thy latter end; And thou say in thine heart, My power and the might of mine hand hath gotten me this wealth. But thou shalt remember the Lord thy God: for it is he that giveth thee power to get wealth, that he may establish his covenant which he sware unto thy fathers, as it is this day" (Deuteronomy 8:11-18).

In May of 1970 we moved to Fort Worth, Texas, to go to work for Brother Kenneth Copeland. I was so far in debt that I could not afford to pay over $100 a month to rent a house. Every dime that came in to me was going out on debts. We found a little wood frame house in a poor neighborhood and moved into it. While I worked at Brother Copeland's office I would confess, "I live the abundant life. I am prosperous in the name of Jesus. I am redeemed from the curse . . ." Then I would get in that *old worn out car* that had over 100,000 miles on it; believe God for it to start and drive back to that little old dump that we lived in.

As I walked into that place, I would get swallowed up in oppression. We didn't have a stove, or a table to eat on, or a refrigerator. All we had was junk. *It seemed as though all the poverty demons of hell would gang up, as they waited for me to get off work, to welcome me home and say, "Come on in, Jerry, we've been waiting for you."*

I would walk in there and tell Carolyn, "In the name of Jesus of Nazareth, we are not staying in this place. God is going to deliver us." And He did! Progressively we began to prosper. At the time of this writing we live in the finest home that we have ever owned. It has over 5000 square feet of living space and we are enjoying every inch of it. I shall never forget that God is my source, and He has redeemed me from the curse of poverty. And as long as I keep this in sight, my heart will never be lifted up in pride.

If You Maintain A Balance There Will Be No Limitations

As long as you remember that it is the Lord your God who has redeemed you from poverty, and has given you the power to get riches, you will not have to worry about going to the extreme. The devil is waiting for you to open the door through the deceitfulness of riches so he can destroy you. When you begin to realize that God will go with you as far as you want to go in prosperity, and you do not allow yourself to be lifted up in pride, there are no limitations. The balance comes when you know that God is your source.

Jesus said, "Thy will be done on earth as it is in heaven." There is no limit to how prosperous the believer can live on this earth if he will keep in sight the fact that it is the Almighty God who has helped him and delivered him. It is God who gives him the power to get wealth.

If You Are A Believer You Are "Somebody"

You should realize that without Him you are nothing; but if you have Him, then know that *you can do all things through Christ who strengthens you. You are a child of the living God, a joint heir with Jesus Christ, and the redeemed of the Lord.* That makes you "somebody."

The Bible says, "Let the redeemed of the Lord say so." You are redeemed, hallelujah! You have a right to live a prosperous life.

Be One Of The Rare Kind

Don't just follow the crowd that says, "God loves poverty." Break away from traditions that make God's Word of no effect. Dare to step out. Be one of the rare kind who refuses to be defeated.

I wish every believer would make this decision, "From now on I am going to prosper. I am going to set my goals and follow the instructions that God has set forth in His Word, and I refuse to be defeated."

It grieves me to say this, but there are several couples who heard the Word of faith the same hour that Carolyn and I heard it in 1969. They sat in the same place that we sat, and some of them were in the same condition that we were when we heard it. But we were one of the only couples who stuck to it. Many of them have now come back, but they have missed out on a lot of blessings because they did not stay in the Word.

God did not select me out of that group and say, "Jerry, you have what it takes." I did not have what it took, but I was determined to get it. God developed those things in me as I got into His Word.

There are many Christians who want prosperity. Some of them will not receive it. But there are some of those rare kind who will get it. I have watched some of the people who have worked with me in this ministry during the years and I can always spot those rare kind. They're the ones who can't get enough of the Word.

There was a young man that worked with me at one time, and every time I looked at him I saw Jerry Savelle just a few years ago. I saw myself when he came to work in that old car with the banged up front-end. He had made God his source and was believing for prosperity. I never saw him without the Word of God. Once I watched as he was cleaning my office. He had on a headset and a tape recorder strapped around his waist. As he worked, he was filling his spirit with the Word of God and confessing it out of his mouth.

Not long ago he sat in the car with me and said, "Brother Jerry, I appreciate you so much. I just want you to know how much it means to me to observe your uncompromising stand on God's Word. I just want you to know how much it means to me to just be able to sit under your ministry." He said, "I want wisdom. I know your testimony, and I know where you came from. I know where you are headed. That is what I desire. I have put the Word of God first place in my life."

He is one of the *rare kind*. He will make it. It will not take this young man as long to succeed as it took me, if he continues to give the Word first place. There is so much revelation knowledge available to people today, more than there was several years ago. It will not take those *rare kind* forty years to enjoy success.

I thank God for people like Brother Kenneth E. Hagin who stood for forty years, paving the way and digging out nuggets of truth for those of us who are coming up behind him. Now is a good time for you to be one of the *rare kind*. The *rare kind* are *those who constantly dig in the Word of God. They have the desire that it takes to win.* There are some who have the desire, but they will not meet the conditions. They will not determine within themselves to win.

Be one of the rare kind.

16
Learn to Give

I had been teaching on prosperity at *Overcoming Faith Center* every Sunday for approximately five weeks when the Spirit of God said to me, *"Just keep teaching this and I'll continue to reveal spiritual truths to you."* He said, *"I want you to create a prosperous atmosphere, because I want everybody in this church to prosper."*

It really turns me on when the people begin to prosper, and the Lord is blessing the work of their hand. There have been several people come to the church who were in financial need. Some of them were just visiting, and we had never seen them before. Often the Spirit of God would instruct me to have the congregation bring their offerings up to the altar, and then invite everybody who had a financial need to come up and get what they needed. One particular night the anointing of God was very strong as I specifically taught on giving. We got into some new things that I had never taught before. There seemed to be a spirit of giving that came upon the service. The Bible tells us that the apostle Paul prayed that God would grant unto you the spirit of wisdom. Well, why not a spirit of giving? You see, there is a spirit of giving, and the spirit of giving came on the people that night.

The Spirit of God said, "Now, I want you to receive an offering." It would not be right to teach on prosperity and not allow the people an opportunity to give. That would be like teaching on healing and then not praying for the sick. He said, "I want you to have them bring it up to the altar and place all of their gifts on the table; then invite everybody who has a financial need to come and get whatever they need."

Praise God! We gave away almost $2,000 that night to people in need. One fellow said, "I needed $455 by 9:00 o'clock in the morning or I would have been put out of my house."

One night Bill Basansky was with us at *Overcoming Faith Center* in our *Believer's Rally*. The Spirit of God spoke to both of us and told us to have a young black man in the audience come up and give his testimony. We were inviting people to give their testimonies concerning things that had happened to them during the rally that week. A lady in our church works for a born again, Spirit-filled psychiatrist. The psychiatrist often sends his patients to our church and he had sent this black man to us. The man had been in a lot of trouble — in jail, and in several mental institutions. He stood up and told how the Lord had blessed him that night, and that he had never been in a place like that before. In fact, he had never heard of *Overcoming Faith Center* before, until his psychiatrist had suggested that he attend the services there.

At that moment, the Spirit of God prompted Bill and me to receive an offering for the man. I invited the people to come up and put the money in his hands. I said, "I want you to fill his pockets up!" The people brought the money to the man. My father, who works with me in the ministry, counted it. There was over $800. The man then told us that he had all kinds of financial needs, and that his wife was to the point that she did not know what to do.

I thought, "Dear Lord! I would like to go home with that man tonight." Don't you know his wife was surprised?

We have fun with our giving. We have learned to be cheerful about it. The Word says: "Every man according as he purposeth in his heart, so let him give; not grudgingly, or of necessity: for God loveth a cheerful giver" (2 Corinthians 9:7). We have found this to be true: ". . . remember the words of the Lord Jesus, how he said, It is more blessed to give than to receive" (Acts 20:35). It is a pleasure to give.

If somebody had not taught me the law of giving, I would still be in the shape that I was in, or even worse. We have given our way out of debt. We have given our way out of the low-life. We are living the high-life! Praise God!

Please, do not misunderstand. When I talk about prosperity, I do not want to give the impression that I have bags full of money everywhere, and that I no longer have to use my faith because I have so much money. *Many people think that if a preacher does not come in squalling and bawling, talking their needs and conning the people with some kind of gimmick or trick, he is just rolling in money.* That is not true. God is my source and when I need finances I know how to go to Him in faith.

When I was still working with Brother Kenneth Copeland, I heard a man say to him once, "Brother Copeland, the way you talk you must have truck loads of money coming to your office all the time."

Brother Copeland said, "No, but you just keep confessing that, and I'll agree with it, praise God!"

I am saying this: God has honored our giving. Our ministry has been blessed because we are givers.

Giving does not always involve just money. Giving is a principle that is going to cause you to prosper in every area.

If you need love, give love.

If you need friends, be friendly.

If you need time, give time.

When you become a giver in every area of your life, there is no way that the devil can stop you from prospering in every area of your life. Giving is very important for prosperity. If you do not give, you will not prosper. You will limit yourself.

When I first started in this ministry, the Spirit of God instructed me to put our messages on tape. I thought, "Dear Lord, I don't even like them. Why would anybody else want to buy our tapes?"

I said, "Well, Lord, I am going to put the messages on tape because You instructed me to." Then I started giving. I gave tapes to prisons, to various ministries, to teen challenge groups, and to people who couldn't afford to purchase them. We just gave until it looked like there was just no way to give any more; but God blessed our giving and our tape ministry is blessed. The demand for our tapes is at a greater level today than it has ever been. There is no other reason for this than because we are givers.

"Give, and it shall be given unto you; good measure, pressed down, and shaken together, and running over, shall men give into your bosom. For with the same measure that ye mete withal it shall be measured to you again" (Luke 6:38).

Make this verse a practical application in your life. You will find that you will never be able to outgive God.

17
Learn to Receive

You might as well learn right now: *if you intend to prosper, you are going to have to become a giver*. Once you learn to give it is equally important that you learn to receive. Sometimes, learning to receive is harder than learning to give.

There was a fellow in our church who at one time was a very wealthy businessman. By the world's standards he was on top. He had it all going for him, but he was running from God as fast as he could run and he lost every dime of it. Satan stole it from him.

Not long after he lost his wealth he came to Fort Worth and received Jesus as his Lord. Not too long afterwards he began attending our church. The first message that he heard me preach was entitled *"Prosperity of the Soul."* I said, "If you want to prosper financially according to 3 John 2, you must prosper in your soul first." This message witnessed to his spirit. He and his wife began attending *Overcoming Faith Center* regularly. They began to grow in the Word and God was working with them and blessing them. They eventually became very faithful workers in the church.

He Had To Learn To Receive

Because that man had been on top at one time, and he was used to having plenty of money, it was hard for him to receive. Once a young man walked up to him and handed him five dollars. The man backed up and said, "I can't take that." Right at that moment he was needing money desperately. He had very little food for his family.

The young man said, "God told me to give you this five dollars." After the man refused to take the money, the young man came to me and said, "Brother Jerry, I don't understand. I am trying to give and that man won't receive. He is blocking my blessing."

I went to the man and said, "You had better learn how to receive."

He said, "No! I just can't do that."

"What are you going to do, shut God off?" I said. "Aren't you praying and asking God to meet your needs? How do you think He is going to do that?"

"Well," he said, "I just can't take money from that kid. He probably needs that money worse than I do."

I said, "He probably does. That is the reason that he was going to give it to you."

It took that man a while to understand that he was going to have to learn to receive. *Pride* was keeping him from receiving. PRIDE! I want you to know that *when he got rid of that pride, he learned how to receive and God blessed him.*

Don't Shut The Door On God

If you cannot receive from your brothers or sisters, you will not be able to receive from God. Many times that is the avenue that God chooses to get your needs met. It is not His only avenue. He can use a raven; He can use a fish; He can use a dog; and He can use a mule.

People are not God's only source. He can use any avenue that He desires, but when you start shutting God's avenues off, you are shutting God off. In order for you to enjoy prosperity in your life, you must not only learn to give but you must learn to receive.

18
Occupy

In the 19th chapter of Luke, Jesus gives us a parable. We read in verses 11-13: "And as they heard these things, he added and spake a parable, because he was nigh to Jerusalem, and because they thought that the kingdom of God should immediately appear. He said therefore, A certain nobleman went into a far country to receive for himself a kingdom, and to return. And he called his ten servants, and delivered them ten pounds, and said unto them, *Occupy till I come.*" You will notice in verse 13, the nobleman said, "Occupy till I come." The word *occupy* literally means "to enter into transactions; do business;" or in one sense of the word, *to trade.* You will note that he distributed ten pounds among his servants, and instructed them to do something with them.

We read in Matthew 25:14-21 an account of the same parable.

"For the kingdom of heaven is as a man travelling into a far country, who called his own servants, and delivered unto them his goods.

"And unto one he gave five talents, to another two, and to another one; to every man according to his several ability; and straightway took his journey.

"Then he that had received the five talents went and traded with the same, and made them other five talents.

"And likewise he that had received two, he also gained other two.

"But he that had received one went and digged in the earth, and hid his lord's money.

"After a long time the lord of those servants cometh, and reckoneth with them.

"And so he that had received five talents came and brought other five talents, saying, Lord, thou deliveredst unto me five talents: behold, I have gained beside them five talents more.

"His lord said unto him, Well done, thou good and faithful servant: thou hast been faithful over a few things, I will make thee ruler over many things: enter thou into the joy of thy lord."

We read in verse 20 where the servant who received five talents came and brought five other talents, saying, "Lord, you gave me five talents, I have gained five talents more . . . ." Evidently *this servant occupied:* he entered into some kind of transaction. And the man said to him, "Well done, thou good and faithful servant. You have been faithful over a few things, I will make you a ruler over many . . . ." (v. 21) Jesus is saying to us that it makes no difference what we have obtained: wealth, honor, whatever; God is the source. God is the Author of any talents, special ability, or gift that we may have.

Many people do not recognize or acknowledge that God is the Author of prosperity. This is the reason that the Bible says that it is dangerous for a man to say, "By my own hand I got this wealth." Without God man could not become prosperous. God distributes to His people — He is the source.

Somebody asks, "Why is it that some people seem to be more prosperous?"

Some are highly motivated, and some are not. The highly motivated ones get into the Word; do the Word; meditate the Word; act on the Word. God is going to reward them for it.

When that one servant took his talents that the nobleman had given him and told him to *occupy*, he put them to work and they worked for him. And his master said, "Well done, thou good and faithful servant, you have been faithful over a few things, and I will make you a ruler over many. Enter into the joy of your lord."

Evidently, occupying (getting involved; getting in on the giving end with that which God has blessed you with) will cause you to enter into the joy of the Lord. When you are a giver, you know that you have a covenant with God, and that Jesus is the guarantee of that covenant, you can enter into the joy of the Lord, regardless of how desperate it looks. Why? Because God's Word works. It brings joy.

Don't Wait For A Crisis Before You Start Giving

As a Christian you should have a giving nature. You should not wait until a financial need or a great crisis arises, and then say, "The Word says, 'Give, and it shall be given unto me (you) . . .' I guess I had better give something quickly!"

Many times if you wait until the last five minutes when you are under pressure and then start giving, you have waited almost too late. Become a giver when there is no crisis. Get it working for you all the time. Then when a crisis comes, you can still enter into the joy of the Lord, because you know you have already occupied. Spiritual law is out there working for you.

Somebody said, "Well, I'll wait until I have more money to give." You will never have more until you start giving. If you only have a nickel start with that nickel, and believe that God will increase it. He said that the servant was a faithful servant because he occupied. Be faithful and start with what you have.

We will continue reading the parable in Matthew 25 and read verses 22-30: *"He also that had received two talents came and said, Lord, thou deliveredst unto me two talents: behold, I have gained two other talents beside them.*
"His lord said unto him, Well done, good and faithful servant; thou hast been faithful over a few things, I will make thee ruler over many things: enter thou into the joy of thy lord.
"Then he which had received the one talent came and said, Lord, I knew thee that thou art an hard man, reaping where thou hast not sown, and gathering where thou hast not strawed:
"And I was afraid, and went and hid thy talent in the earth: lo, there thou hast that is thine.

"His lord answered and said unto him, Thou wicked and slothful servant, thou knewest that I reap where I sowed not, and gather where I have not strawed:

"Thou oughtest therefore to have put my money to the exchangers, and then at my coming I should have received mine own with usury.

"Take therefore the talent from him, and give it unto him which hath ten talents.

"For unto every one that hath shall be given, and he shall have abundance: but from him that hath not shall be taken away even that which he hath.

"And cast ye the unprofitable servant into outer darkness: there shall be weeping and gnashing of teeth."

TWO OF THOSE SERVANTS OCCUPIED. THEY BECAME INVOLVED; THEY WERE FAITHFUL SERVANTS. The other did nothing and therefore did not prosper. What will you do?

Fear Activates The Devil Like Faith Activates God

You can see also that one servant was afraid. He became gripped with fear. Many Christians become gripped with fear. They will hold on to that last dime that they have because they are afraid that they will lose it. They will say, "Brother! this is all I have; these are hard times, and I don't expect to be getting any more money real soon."

If you do this, you are operating in fear and you have opened the door to the devil. When this happens you have become an unfaithful servant. He called the man who did not *occupy*, "a wicked and slothful servant."

The Bible does not say, "Follow those who are wicked and slothful." It says, "Follow those who through faith and patience enter into the promises, or receive the promises of God." It also says, "We want you to show the same diligence and be not slothful." Slothfulness is *spiritual laziness*, and *spiritual laziness* will get you into trouble. It will bring you into poverty quickly. When you realize that God is your source, and that He is the Author of every good and perfect gift, and all of the substance that you now have is because of God, then you become faithful with that substance. You will become as the good and faithful servants. God can trust you with an abundance. He that has been faithful, shall have abundance. He that is slothful — *spiritually lazy*, he shall be defeated.

You Do Not Have To Be Defeated

To live an undefeated life you must do something with your substance. You must become a giver. However, there is wisdom needed in giving. You must keep your Word level up as you become a giver. We talked about this in another chapter of this book. If you say, "Well, Brother Jerry said, 'Be a giver,' " and you run out and give your car away, that is not using wisdom. If I told you that I gave my car away and God gave me a brand new El Dorado Cadillac, you might think that is what you should do because I told you what happened to me: that may not be wisdom. I didn't give my car away just because I heard somebody else tell me that they gave their car away. *I didn't give my car away until my Word level was up to the point when I knew that I knew that if I gave it away I was going to get another one.* There was no doubt in my mind or heart. I did not do it just "trying something." I went to the Word of God and fed my spirit, and the Word prompted me to give.

I repeat: Don't go out and just give everything away because someone else did. I am not going to give unless I am prompted by the Word or the Spirit of God.

Where you give is also important. You can tithe in the wrong place and destroy the effect of your tithing. The Bible tells us not to put our tithe in a dead work. That would be like the farmer who took his seed and spread it out on a concrete parking lot. He cannot expect to reap a good harvest if the seed is on a parking lot. The seed you plant must go into good soil.

Somebody said, "Well, I have been tithing to this church ever since I became a Christian."

Are they preaching the Word?

"Well, we have a good visitation program."

Are they producing? Is there a harvest?

Putting your money into something that is dead is just as stupid as buying tomato seeds and tossing them out on a parking lot. You have wasted your money. The seed will not produce if it is not planted in good soil. Plant your seed in a good soil. Pray and ask God to reveal to you where to plant your seed. *Get into the*

Word of God, and allow the Holy Spirit to show you how to invest your money wisely.

Above all, be faithful and God will make you ruler over much.

19
Become a Faithful Steward

God is in business in this earth, and He wants a lot of partners. He needs faithful stewards. God's business is saving souls, healing bodies, and delivering people from satan's bondage. You can become a co-worker with God. You will never enter into any kind of partnership that pays the kind of dividends that God pays. His returns are good! Do you know anyone who is wiser or wealthier than God?

The Bible says in Deuteronomy 8:18, "But thou shalt remember the Lord thy God: for it is he that giveth thee power to get wealth, that he may establish his covenant which he sware unto thy fathers, as it is this day." If it is God who gives you power to get wealth in order to establish His covenant, then you should become a good steward over that wealth. God desires faithful stewards. The Bible says, "Let a man so account of us, as of the ministers of Christ, and stewards of the mysteries of God. Moreover it is required in stewards, that a man be found faithful" (1 Corinthians 4:1, 2). The word *faithful* means "trustworthy; honest; dependable; loyal; consistent; truthful; full of faith; steadfast; diligent, and disciplined." The inconsistent giver, the undisciplined giver, or the giver who is lacking in trust is not a faithful giver. The faithful steward, the dependable, diligent giver is the one whom God can count on.

I Was Not Always A Faithful Steward

It gives me great pleasure knowing that many times the Spirit of God has passed over one hundred men who would not listen, and then call on me and say: "I want you to give."

I have said, "Father, here am I. Speak on . . . ." It has not always been that way. I remember once when I was working with Brother Kenneth Copeland. I was preparing to go to North Carolina for a faith seminar. While I was getting ready for the trip, the Lord said to me, "Before you leave town I want you to send Joe Nay (a minister friend of mine) some money."

I said, "All right, Lord, I'll do that."

I kept on packing. He stopped me and said again, "I want you to send Joe that money."

I said, "All right, Lord. I'll do that just as soon as I finish packing. I will write a check and get it in the mail to him."

I kept on working, and then left Fort Worth. As I was driving down the freeway listening to the New Testament I heard, "I told you to send that money."

"All right, Lord. I'll do that just as soon as I get to North Carolina." That was stupid. The man only lived a few miles from me in Arlington, Texas, and I decided to drive all the way to North Carolina and mail the check back to him. When I arrived in Memphis to rest for the night, I heard it once again: "I told you to send Joe that money. Now get up and do it!" He said, "Call your wife and tell her to get that check in the mail tonight."

I did as I was told, and when I hung up the phone I said, "Lord, why were You so persistent?"

He said, "Joe needed the money now; he needed it today! Now you have already fouled up and I had to call on somebody else to get it to him." He said, "You are the very one who squalls and bawls when the money arrives a day late when you pray. And do you know why? There are many of My people that are acting just like you. When I tell them to do something, they run all over the country doing everything else. When they 'get time,' they will do it."

He said, "I have a man standing in faith, waiting for his need to be met and you've been running around saying, 'Yes, Lord, I'll do it,' but you never get around to it." He said, "I suggest that you straighten up or I'll just have to call on someone else who will be faithful."

Giving to Joe did not disturb me at all. But I was not faithful to do it at the moment when God told me to do it. That taught me a lesson. There is another law at work: "Do unto others as you would have them do unto you." That is just as much a spiritual law as, "Give, and it shall be given unto you, good measure, pressed down, shaken together, and running over shall men give unto your bosom . . . ." (Author's paraphrase) God does not want you under condemnation about this, but He is telling us that when we become faithful stewards, He can trust us with abundance.

"Moreover, it is required in stewards that a man be found faithful." Become a faithful steward: trustworthy; dependable; consistent, and prompt to do it, without hesitation. Then, the people to whom God speaks concerning your needs will give to you as quickly as you give to others.

20

Storehouses

A familiar passage of Scripture is found in Proverbs 3:9, 10: "Honour the Lord with thy substance, and with the firstfruits of all thine increase: So shall *thy barns* be filled with plenty, and thy presses shall burst out with new wine." He is saying, *"Honor the Lord with the firstfruits of thine increase."* You should become a faithful steward over everything that you have because God is the source of your supply. You should become a faithful steward over your time, your money, your wisdom, your love, your joy — everything that you possess. You must become a faithful steward over everything that God has given to you. You may have the wisdom of God that the man next door needs. Be a faithful steward over that wisdom. Remember: if you are faithful over little, He'll make you ruler over much.

Your Barn Is Your Storehouse

Let's use the word *storehouse* instead of *barn*, and read that Scripture passage again: "Honour the Lord with thy substance, and with the firstfruits of all thine increase; So shall thy *storehouse* be filled with plenty . . . ." A storehouse could be a *savings account*.

He said that if you will honor the Lord with your substance, and the firstfruits of your increase, your barns, or storehouses will be full. Evidently a storehouse is something where one keeps things in reserve that are not necessarily needed at the moment.

Many people have storehouses motivated by fear. This motivation for a storehouse is where you can get into trouble. Some people say, "Well, I am saving for a rainy day. You never know what is out there in the future." *You will get exactly what you believe for.* You will have *rainy days!*

The Lord said to me, "Son, most people think like that in the earth — right now. They accumulate funds because they are afraid of the future." That motivation can destroy you because you open the door to the devil.

How many people do you know whose motivation behind a savings account is because they are afraid? And did you know that everything they fear always happens to them?

There Is A Motivation For A Storehouse That Is Right

There is a storehouse that God will honor. I have a storehouse, but not because I am afraid of the future. I have a storehouse or reservoir for whatever is needed at the time. Sometimes the need is a fellow-believer who has experienced a financial crisis. Instead of saying, "Oh, God, I wish there was something I could do." I can go to my storehouse. God does not mind you having a storehouse. In fact, He said that it would be plenteous.

God talks in terms of abundance. *Plenty* is a word connected to *abundance*. He said, if you will honor Him with all your substance and the firstfruits of your increase, your storehouse (barns) will be filled with plenty. That is God's plan for His people. Not just barely making it, but abundance, plenty, more than enough for your needs, and able to help somebody else.

You Need To Rightly Divide The Scriptures

Some people misinterpret the following Scripture passage: "Lay not up for yourselves treasures upon earth, where moth and rust doth corrupt, and where thieves break through and steal: But lay up for yourselves treasures in heaven, where neither moth nor rust doth corrupt, and where thieves do not break through nor steal: For where your treasure is, there will your heart be also" (Matthew 6:19-21).

Some people will read, "Lay not up for yourselves treasures on earth," and stop right there, and say, "Well, Brother Savelle, we are not supposed to have savings accounts, because that is a treasure upon earth. We are not supposed to have a storehouse."

That is not what He said. There is an explanation in the last verse. ". . . For where your treasure is, there will your heart be also." You can make your savings account that in which you place your trust, and that is when it becomes dangerous. Do not trust in your riches. Your savings account, or your bank account is temporal. In other words, it can change in a moment for good or for bad. He is telling us, "Don't lay up treasures upon earth with the motivation that that is where your heart is going to be." Do not make your storehouse your source of supply. God is your source of supply, and He will bless your storehouse. It is very easy, if you have a large bank account, to begin to depend upon it as your source instead of the Lord.

God's Storehouse

He tells us: "Bring ye all the tithes into the storehouse, that there may be meat in mine house, and prove me now herewith, saith the Lord of hosts, if I will not open you the windows of heaven, and pour you out a blessing, that there shall not be room enough to receive it" (Malachi 3:10). When He says, *"That there may be meat in mine house . . . ."* He is talking about His storehouse. There are times when the Bible uses the word "meat" and it is in reference to spiritual food. Peter said, ". . . desire the sincere milk of the word, that ye may grow thereby" (1 Peter 2:2). The apostle Paul said, "But strong meat belongeth to them that are of full age, even those who by reason of use have their senses exercised to discern both good and evil" (Hebrews 5:14).

When God said, "Bring ye all the tithes into the storehouse, that there may be meat in my house," He was saying that it takes money to feed the people meat (spiritual food). Many churches have had to shut their doors because people did not bring in their tithes and offerings into God's storehouse — so that there could be meat preached without hindrance. If you go to a church and you are fed spiritual meat there, you should support it. That church has become God's storehouse. He said, "Bring the tithes and offerings in, so that there is meat." In other words, when the people are obedient to God and bring their tithes and offerings into the storehouse, then, thank God, they will never have to be concerned about any hindrances.

Tithing Is Not A Product Of The Law

You should be a tither. If you will become a faithful steward and honor the Lord with your substance and the firstfruits of your increase, then you will place yourself in a position to have God's blessings poured out on you in abundance. You are not under the law when you tithe. Tithing was in existence before the law ever came. Abraham tithed to Melchizedek. Tithing came right in the beginning, and it still works today. The children of Israel did not stop at tithing just their money. They brought in one-tenth of all their substance. "And as soon as the commandment came abroad, the children of Israel brought in abundance the firstfruits of corn, wine, and oil, and honey, and of all the increase of the field; and the tithe of all things brought they in abundantly" (2 Chronicles 31:5).

When the word *tithe* is used in the Old Testament, it literally means *"one-tenth."* Most Christians agree that the tithe is one-tenth of the income. If you make $1,000 a month and you are a faithful steward, you will bring $100 into God's storehouse. You may say, "Now, wait a minute! I make $1,000 but I only bring home $842." I still suggest that you take it off the top and tithe $100. "Yes, but if I take it off the top I won't have enough." If you are faithful, God will cause you to have plenty.

Don't let the devil tell you that this is not for Christians today. He is only trying to rob you of a tremendous blessing.

21

Learning to Use Your Faith

I was riding in an automobile with a very successful businessman some years ago, and he asked me this question: "Now, what I want to know is this: do you mean to tell me that you just believe God for everything you need?"

"Well, sure!" I said.

He asked, "If you have the money to just go out and buy it, do you use your faith or your money?"

I said, "Let me share this with you. I live by faith. Many times I do it this way — I will use my faith just for the practice." Then I gave him this example.... I once walked into a Baptist Book Store in Fort Worth, Texas, and they has an *Interlinear Greek New Testament* that I wanted. The price was about ten dollars, and I had the money in my pocket to buy it. As I started to take the book from the shelf the Spirit of God said to me, "Son, you need some practice. The same principle that will produce a ten dollar Bible will produce a ten thousand dollar piece of equipment. Don't wait until you need the ten thousand dollar item before you learn to use your faith." I laid my hand on that Bible and said, "In the name of Jesus of Nazareth, I believe I receive a Bible just like this according to Mark 11:24." I walked out of that book store, and, of course, the clerk thought that I was *nuts!*

I went back to the office. I heard a man come into the office and ask, "Is Jerry Savelle here?" The receptionist told him that I was back in the tape room and that he could come back and see me. That man walked into the room with two Bibles under his arms. I could tell by the color of the covers that they were *Interlinear Greek New Testaments*.

"Are you believing for a Bible?" He asked.

"Yes!" I said.

He said, "I was in the Baptist Book Store just a few minutes ago. I reached for one of these Bibles to buy for myself, and God said, 'Buy two of them and give one to Jerry Savelle.' "

After I related that experience to this businessman, I said, "Now, I did that for practice. I had the money, but you can see how that inspired my faith. That tells me that my faith can produce whatever I need whether I have the money or not."

My Faith Is At Work Constantly

Regardless of the price of the item that you are in need of, the principle works just the same. Do not wait until the need is already upon you and then start trying to develop your faith. Get your faith working now. The just shall live by faith.

WHO IS YOUR SOURCE?

Jesus said, "Lay not up for yourselves treasures upon earth, where moth and rust doth corrupt . . . . For where your treasure is, there will your heart be also." You must never allow your bank account to become your source. Let God be your source, and He will increase your bank account. Do not put your dependence upon your storehouse, even if it is bursting with plenty and abundance. If you will keep God as your source, there is no limit to the abundance to that storehouse. I repeat: It is so important that you do not allow your storehouse — your bank account — your substance to be your source of supply.

We read in Mark 10:17-20, "And when he was gone forth into the way, there came one running, and kneeled to him, and asked him, Good Master, what shall I do that I may inherit eternal life? And Jesus said unto him, Why callest thou me good? There is none good but one, that is, God. Thou knowest the commandments, Do not commit adultery, Do not kill, Do not steal, Do not bear false witness, Defraud not, Honour thy father and mother. And he answered and said unto him, Master, all these have I observed from my youth."

You will remember that God said in Deuteronomy 8:18, ". . . it is he (God) that giveth thee power to get wealth . . . ." You see, the man we are reading about in Mark 10 was a rich man. He had great wealth. He asked Jesus what he could do to inherit eternal life. Jesus told him, "You know the commandments." And the man told Jesus that he had kept all of them since his youth. That was the reason why the man was rich. He had been operating the covenant. He had been operating the principles of the law. And because of that, God had made him wealthy.

One could become wealthy under the Old Covenant in that day. Provision was made for financial prosperity under the Old Covenant. That man who came to Jesus was operating under that Old Covenant. He kept the law and because of that, he became a wealthy person. Notice what Jesus told him. ". . . One thing thou lackest: go thy way, sell whatsoever thou hast, and give to the poor, and thou shalt have treasure in heaven: and come, take up the cross, and follow me." (v. 21) Many people will read that and put religious ideas into it. They say that Jesus doesn't want Christians to have anything; that you can't serve God and have things.

They are wording it wrong. *It is hard to serve God when things have you.* You can have things, but you must not allow things to have you. Jesus is not telling the rich man that he cannot possess things. That would be contradictory to what Proverbs said: "Honour the Lord with thy substance . . . ."

Jesus simply said, "There is one thing that you are lacking . . . ." He is suggesting to the man that he should do something to correct the thing that he is lacking. Jesus said, ". . . sell whatsoever thou hast, and give to the poor, and thou shalt have treasure in heaven: and come, take up the cross, and follow me. And he was sad at that saying, and went away grieved: for he had great possessions. And Jesus looked round about, and saith unto his disciples, How hardly shall they that have riches enter into the kingdom of God! And the disciples were astonished at his words. But Jesus answereth again, and saith unto them, Children, how hard is it for them that trust in riches to enter into the kindgom of God!" (vv. 21b-24) Jesus was trying to get the man delivered of trusting in his riches. God had blessed the man and prospered him, but the man had made his riches his source, instead of trusting in God as his source. Jesus is saying, "It is hard for them who trust in riches to enter into the kingdom of God."

God wants you to have a storehouse. He wants you to be blessed financially, but He does not want you to allow your storehouse, your bank account, your finances, or your material things to become your source. If you do, there will come a time in your life when you will not have enough; no matter how much you have it will not meet the need.

When God is totally your source there is no limit to what He will do with your storehouse. "The Lord shall command the blessing upon thee in thy storehouses, and in all that thou settest thine hand unto; and he shall bless thee in the land which the Lord thy God giveth thee" (Deuteronomy 28:8).

22

If You're Faithful to God's Storehouse, He is Faithful to Yours

Matthew 25:21 says, ". . . thou good and faithful servant: thou hast been faithful over a few things, I will make thee ruler over many things: enter thou into the joy of thy lord." God is not trying to strip you of things. He wants you to put your trust in Him. As you do, there is no limit to the things that will come as a result. God is saying that if you will honor Him or be faithful with your substance, He will cause your storehouse to have plenty. You shall have abundance. He will make you ruler over much.

We read in Malachi 3:8-12, "Will a man rob God? Yet ye have robbed me. But ye say, Wherein have we robbed thee? In tithes and offerings. Ye are cursed with a curse: for ye have robbed me, even this whole nation. Bring ye all the tithes into the storehouse, that there may be meat in mine house, and prove me now herewith, saith the Lord of hosts, if I will not open you the windows of heaven, and pour you out a blessing, that there shall not be room enough to receive it. And I will rebuke the devourer for your sakes, and he shall not destroy the fruits of your ground; neither shall your vine cast her fruit before the time in the field, saith the Lord of hosts. And all the nations shall call you blessed: for ye shall be a delightsome land, saith the Lord of hosts."

Please notice, that is God talking in the above Scripture passage. He is telling you to bring all of your tithes into His storehouse, that there may be meat in His house. He is not referring to your storehouse or my storehouse; *He is referring to His storehouse.*

God refers to our storehouse in Deuteronomy 28: "Blessed shall be thy basket and thy store. Blessed shalt thou be when thou comest in, and blessed shalt thou be when thou goest out. The Lord shall cause thine enemies that rise up against thee to be smitten before thy face: they shall come out against thee one way, and flee before thee seven ways. *The Lord shall command the blessing upon thee in thy storehouses,* and in all that thou settest thine hand unto; and he shall bless thee in the land which the Lord thy God giveth thee." (vv. 5-8) When you begin to enter into a faithful stewardship with God's storehouse, He will command the blessings upon you and your storehouse. He will also rebuke the devourer for you.

Can you imagine what it must sound like to the devil when God rebukes him? Can you imagine what authority is exercised when God says, "I command the blessing on Jerry Savelle's storehouse." All the angels stand at attention, and they will move immediately to get that money into my storehouse. All of hell trembles until God's voice is heard no more. The Bible says that His voice is like the sound of many waters. I have stood at Niagara Falls and listened to the roar of that rushing water. It is a magnificent sound. You can hear it for miles. It is almost impossible to imagine what God's rebuke would sound like.

Do You Have A Storehouse?

God wants you to have a storehouse. When you become faithful to His storehouse, He will be faithful to yours. I discovered this when the Spirit of God said to me, "Son, there is an avenue of prosperity that I have not been able to do anything about with you."

I said, "Why not?"

He said, "Because you do not have a storehouse."

I said, "You are right." There was a time when I thought it was wrong to save money. I thought God did not want me to have anything just sitting in a bank account. I had read over in Matthew chapter 6 where it says, "Do not lay up treasures upon the earth . . ." and I thought, "Well, that settles it. You are not supposed to have anything in reserve."

The Spirit of God began to deal with me concerning this, and He said, "Son, your storehouse is something that is not needed right at the moment, it is on hand when needed." In business you might call it capital reserve. He said, "The only thing I am against is your putting your trust in it. I am not against you having a storehouse." Then He told me how to start this. I give one-tenth of my income to God's storehouse, and I started doing the same to my storehouse. I just put one-tenth of my income into His, and one-tenth in mine. This gave me a starting point and God has blessed it tremendously.

Please let me say this: I cannot go to the Bible and give you scriptures for my putting one-tenth of my income into my storehouse. You must understand that this is just a suggestion. I have given you scriptures on God's storehouse and your storehouse, but you will not find it in the Bible that you are to tithe to your storehouse.

The reason that I did this was because my wife and I needed a base to start from, and we started doing it. Just as some people sign up on one of the Christmas club funds at a bank, they start putting five dollars in that account every week and they save money for Christmas.

When we first married, we tried to set aside a few dollars every week and we just could not stick with it. We would get two hundred dollars saved up and then we would take all of it out of the bank but five dollars, just enough to keep the account open. Of course, our motive was not based on the Word of God. I was doing it because I grew up thinking that you are supposed to pay house notes, buy groceries and open savings accounts. Of course, my thinking was that my savings account was supposed to be there to take care of those crisis experiences that I was bound to have.

After we realized that God really wanted to bless our storehouse we began to ask Him how to operate in this with wisdom. We were already tithing into God's storehouse, and we said, "In the name of Jesus, whatever we do with Your storehouse, we are going to match it in our storehouse." We set our faith on that.

When our salary check came in, we made out the check for our tithe, and a second check went into our storehouse for the same amount. Then we started applying the Word of God. I said, "Now, God, Your Word says to prove You in this. I have brought my tithe to Your storehouse and You said that You would open the windows of heaven and pour out a blessing that there would not be room to receive it. You also said that You would bless my storehouse and that You would command a blessing on my storehouse. Now, I have placed my money into my storehouse and I do not have my trust in it; I am not saving for a rainy day. I am creating a storehouse that You will bless and command a blessing upon it. Now, in the name of Jesus, I am going to be consistent with this and I am expecting You to not only bless the return off of my tithes and offerings, but I am expecting You to command the blessings on my storehouse." Those blessings started coming in!

We are givers. We give to people, ministries, and any place else that God instructs us. We look for avenues in which we can give.

When I go by the bank to place my check in my storehouse account, I say, "Father, in the name of Jesus, I just want You to know that I thank You for commanding the blessing on my storehouse."

I remember on one occasion we were having dinner with some friends and the man said, "This is for you and not for the ministry." He gave me a check in the amount of $500. I said, "Thank You, Father, for commanding the blessing on my storehouse." There was no particular need for the money at that time, and the Lord said to me, "Son, that is for your storehouse."

We not only use a storehouse personally, but we also have started doing this in our ministry. Not long ago, we needed a $6,500 typewriter, and for the first time in our ministry, we had the money in the storehouse to go down and pay cash for it without digging into the general operating expenses of the ministry.

As I said, matching the amount of money that you tithe to God's storehouse is only a suggestion. But your storehouse is a part of prosperity. God cannot bless you in that area unless you have a storehouse. Since we have started our storehouse account, the ministry, as well as my wife and I personally, are prospering in a greater way than we ever have before. We have set a goal for the amount of money we desire to have in our storehouse by the end of the year. But remember this: we are not hoarding up. If a need comes to us, we will give to that need from our storehouse. Giving is the way that prosperity comes.

The Lord once said to me, "Son, if you will continue to operate this principle and let me command a blessing on your storehouse, this is one of the ways that you will eventually get into the position where you will owe no man anything but to love him. You will be able to lend and not borrow."

God's Word works. Put it to work in your life today. *Set these goals:*

I WILL MEET THE CONDITIONS THAT GOD HAS PLACED IN HIS WORD.

I WILL FIND, LAY HOLD, AND RETAIN GOD'S WISDOM.

I WILL BECOME A FAITHFUL STEWARD.

I WILL BE FAITHFUL TO GOD'S STOREHOUSE.

I WILL ALWAYS LET GOD BE MY SOURCE.